Reel Canada

Integrated Skills through Canadian Film

Mohammad Hashemi

OXFORD
UNIVERSITY PRESS

OXFORD
UNIVERSITY PRESS

Oxford University Press is a department of the University of Oxford.

It furthers the University's objective of excellence in research, scholarship, and education by publishing worldwide. Oxford is a registered trade mark of Oxford University Press in the UK and in certain other countries.

Published in Canada by
Oxford University Press
8 Sampson Mews, Suite 204,
Don Mills, Ontario M3C 0H5 Canada

www.oupcanada.com

Library and Archives Canada Cataloguing in Publication

Hashemi, Mohammad, 1969–
Reel Canada : integrated skills through Canadian film / Mohammad Hashemi.

(Culture link)
Has supplement: Reel Canada workbook.

ISBN 978-0-19-544442-1

1. English language--Textbooks for second language learners. 2. Readers--Motion pictures--Canada.
3. Readers (Adult). I. Title. II. Series: Culture link

PE1128.H386 2012   428.6'4   C2011-901416-5

Cover image: © 2008 Julie Roy & Michèle Bélanger. All rights reserved.
Image courtesy of the National Film Board of Canada.

Oxford University Press is committed to our environment. This book is printed on Forest Stewardship Council® certified paper and comes from responsible sources.

Printed and bound in Canada.

1 2 3 4 — 15 14 13 12

Acknowledgements

By far the largest debt incurred in writing this book is owed to my publishing team at Oxford Canada with special thanks to Jason Tomassini, Cindy Angelini, and Nadine Coderre, whose enthusiasm, hard work, creative ideas, and advice helped transform this book.

My grateful thanks to Penny Rampado at the National Film Board of Canada for researching films and providing invaluable advice and support at different stages of this project.

I would also like to thank my family, friends, students, and colleagues who helped improve *Reel Canada* with their support, encouragement, and insight.

Introduction

Culture Link is a multi-level, communicative, integrated, Canadian ESL series using films, songs, and history as vehicles of second language learning.

As the first book in the Culture Link series, *Reel Canada* brings the appeal of the moving picture to intermediate-level ESL classrooms through ten memorable Canadian documentaries, animations, and experimental films from the National Film Board of Canada.

These short Canadian films are used as the focal points of four-skill lessons that combine sound, vision, and language to engage students in issues of global importance delivered through a Canadian perspective.

Most of the exercises focus on language use and communication in all four skill areas by concentrating on the topics themselves, much the same way students would in a regular academic program.

Each chapter contains the following sections:

Introduction to whet the learners' curiosity and introduce them to the chapter's topic

Two Reading Comprehension Passages, one as a warm-up to the film and the second one as reinforcement of the theme of the film

Grammar dealing with intermediate-level structures through practical usage-oriented exercises that deal with the theme of the chapter

The Film used to improve all skills through a variety of creative activities

Academic and Creative Writing exercises to give students an opportunity to write in both controlled and free styles

Listening comprehension section, with many clips taken from popular CBC programs and podcasts such as *The Link*, *The Current*, and *Spark*.

Idioms and fixed expressions related to the theme of the chapter

Speaking exercises based on the grammar and the theme of the chapter

Canadian Outlook exploring the theme in terms of its Canadian implications, encouraging critical thinking about how different cultures deal with concepts such as health, privacy, risk taking, crime, and racism

The book is designed to make the laborious task of learning a second language easier and more accessible by making it more fun. Please feel free to keep it so by going through the activities and picking and choosing the exercises that work best in the context of your classroom.

Reel Canada is complemented by a workbook, DVD and audio CD pack, and online teacher's resource and answer keys.

The Mad Canadian

Taking Risks: Self-Test

We take different types of risks from the moment we are born until we die. Can you match each picture to the type of risk it represents?

| physical risk | intellectual risk | financial risk | emotional risk | social risk |

1. _____

2. _____

3. _____

4. _____

5. _____

Compare your answers with a classmate's and discuss the following questions:

1. Which type of risk is the easiest for you to take?
2. Which type of risk is the most difficult for you to take?
3. Can you give one example of each type of risk from your own life?

Reading

Warm-Up Questions

1. What does the expression "nothing ventured, nothing gained" mean to you? Do you agree with this expression?
2. What is the biggest risk you are currently facing in your life?
3. Why haven't you taken this risk? What is keeping you from doing it?

Vocabulary

Exercise A

Many authors use synonyms in their text to avoid repetition. We can use the synonyms of words used in text as clues to the meaning of the words we do not know. Find a synonym for each of the following words in the passage on page 4.

toddler: _____   cautious: _____

tolerance: _____   fulfilling: _____

Exercise B

What is sunscreen?

a) an umbrella that protects you against the sun
b) a cream or liquid that protects you against the sun
c) a curtain that protects you against the sun
d) a mirror that reflects the sun

Exercise C

Match the following words to the pictures.

roller coaster	bungee jumping	parachuting

1. _____   2. _____   3. _____

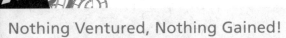

Nothing Ventured, Nothing Gained!

Think back to when you were a kid. How did you learn most of the time? Most people learn about the world around them by taking risks. Babies learn about hot food by eating it. Toddlers always fall while learning to walk. Teenagers learn about their emotions by making and breaking romantic relationships. We have airplanes today because somebody decided to risk it all and build and fly the first one. Almost all progress and advancement happens as a result of risks. As a matter of fact, sometimes the greatest risk is not taking risks.

What you are doing right now might be risky. Are you touching your mouth with unwashed hands? Are you sitting in the sun without wearing sunscreen? Are you sitting next to someone who has a cold? Are you listening to loud music on your headphones as you are reading this book? Taking risks is an essential part of life, but we receive almost no training on how to recognize our risk capacity and how to take good risks and avoid bad ones. In fact, society encourages us to be cautious and not to take risks at all. Our parents tell us, "Be careful, honey!" At school we sometimes lose extra points when we take a wrong guess at a multiple-choice test, but we lose no points when we don't answer. At work our bosses ask us to play it safe. We are taught that any kind of risk that ends up in losing is bad.

We are all different in the amount and types of risks we take. For example, I have a high comfort level with physical or social risks. I love parachuting, bungee jumping, and riding roller coasters. I have no problem talking to a stranger or speaking in public and laughing at myself or being laughed at, but I'm very careful when it comes to lending or borrowing money. Knowing your risk tolerance can help you manage risks better.

It is also very important to take the right risks. A good risk is one that fits the risk taker. It has to be meaningful to the risk taker. Good risks are often fulfilling and they have very clear goals. For example, bungee jumping just to show off to your friends would not be as meaningful and fulfilling as doing it to beat your personal fears.

In the end, taking risks that are right, calculated, and a fit to your personality can be very rewarding. They can make you proud of yourself and improve your life.

Comprehension

1. What is the main idea of this reading passage? Where in the passage can you find the main idea?

2. Underline the sentence that contains the main idea of each paragraph in the passage.

3. What do most teachers, parents, and bosses tell us about risk?

4. What are the characteristics of the right risk?

5. Can you identify the types of risk in the following activities?
    *   making and breaking romantic relationships
    *   learning to walk
    *   flying the first airplane
    *   listening to loud music on your headphones
    *   bungee jumping
    *   talking to a stranger
    *   speaking to a large audience
    *   lending money

Grammar:
Simple Present and Present Progressive

Simple Present

We use the simple present tense when we talk about habits or repeated actions:

> I always **park** my car indoors.

> She **gets** up at six every morning.

We also use the simple present when we talk about facts or timeless truths:

> Normally the heart **beats** 60–100 times per minute.

> Adrenaline **increases** heart rate.

The simple present tense is conjugated in this way:

Affirmative	Negative	Question
I write.	I don't write.	Do I write?
You write.	You don't write.	Do you write?
He/she/it writes.	He/she/it doesn't write.	Does he/she/it write?
We write.	We don't write.	Do we write?
You write.	You don't write.	Do you write?
They write.	They don't write.	Do they write?

Tense Markers

The following tense markers usually come with the simple present tense: adverbs of frequency (*always, never, often*, etc.), *every, once/twice a day/month/week, in the mornings/evenings/afternoons*.

> He goes to the cinema **every weekend**.
> She **always** complains.
> I go there **in the evenings**.

Adverbs of Frequency

Adverbs of frequency show how often something happens.

Here are some common adverbs of frequency:

always, usually, normally, generally, often, frequently, sometimes, occasionally, seldom, rarely, hardly, never

These adverbs mostly come with the simple present tense (repeated action). They normally appear before main verbs and after auxiliary verbs. Some of these adverbs can also be placed at the beginning of the sentence.

Example:

> I **usually** go home at 10.
> I am **usually** home at 10.
> **Usually** I am home at 10.

Present Progressive (Present Continuous)

We use the present progressive (also called present continuous) for an action that is in progress right now.

The present progressive tense is conjugated in this way:

Affirmative	Negative	Question
I am writing.	I'm not writing.	Am I writing?
You are writing.	You aren't writing.	Are you writing?
He/she/it is writing.	He/she/it isn't writing.	Is he/she/it writing?
We are writing.	We aren't writing.	Are we writing?
You are writing.	You aren't writing.	Are you writing?
They are writing.	They aren't writing.	Are they writing?

Tense Markers

The following tense markers usually come with the present progessive tense: *now, at the moment, presently.*

I am watching TV now.

I am presently studying English.

At the moment, I am not doing anything.

Note: We use the simple present tense for verbs of state (verbs that involve no action) even when they are happening right now.

Example:

I know the answer now. (~~I am knowing the answer now.~~)
I see better now. (~~I am seeing better now.~~)

Here are some common verbs of state:

understand	love	hear	exist
believe	like	seem	belong
need	hate	sound	look like

Note: Some verbs can be used both as verbs of action and verbs of state. Such verbs take -*ing* when they are used as verbs of action, but don't take –*ing* when they are verbs of state.

Examples:

He smells good. (state)

He is smelling the flowers. (action)

He looks nice in the picture. (state)

He is looking at the nice picture. (action)

Here are some more verbs that can be used as both action and state verbs with different meanings

think	forget
have	feel
appear	imagine
see	

Exercise A

Go back to the passage "Nothing Ventured, Nothing Gained." Underline all the positive verbs in simple present and present progressive and change them to negative.

Exercise B

Fill in the blanks with the correct present tense of the verbs in parentheses.

At the moment, I $_1$ _____ (sit) in my English class and I $_2$ _____ (try) to do this grammar exercise. Most of my classmates $_3$ _____ (do) the same exercise. There is a student near me who usually $_4$ _____ (not pay) any attention in class. Right now, she $_5$ _____ (check) a message on her cellphone. Almost every day, she $_6$ _____ (leave) her phone on in class and $_7$ _____ (start) playing with it as soon as the teacher $_8$ _____ (be) busy with others, and even when the teacher $_9$ _____ (notice) and $_{10}$ _____ (ask) what she $_{11}$ _____ (do), she $_{12}$ _____ (tell) a lie. For example, she $_{13}$ _____ (say), "I $_{14}$ _____ (look up) a word on my phone's dictionary." This $_{15}$ _____ (distract) me all the time. Normally, I $_{16}$ _____ (not be) a complainer, but this is too much. Now, I $_{17}$ _____ (think) I should talk to the teacher about her behaviour.

Grammar Reinforcement

Game: Spot the Lie

Oral: Work in teams of two. Make five statements about yourself. Four of them are true and one is a lie. Your partner should spot the lie and tell you which one it is. If your partner spots the lie, he or she gets a turn and this time you have to spot the lie.

The Film: *The Mad Canadian*

Video Vocabulary

All the words below are related to the video you are going to watch. In teams of two, go over the list to see how many of the words you have heard before. Check your dictionary for those you don't know.

adrenaline	fire extinguisher	slam	stuntman
cast	motivate	sprain	swollen
constable	overshoot	stock car	touchdown
crew	ramp	stunt	undershoot

Fill in the blanks with the correct form of the words from the list above.

1. Some actors such as Jackie Chan prefer to do most of their own _____ while others employ a _____ to do them.

2. I don't like Formula 1 racing. I prefer _____ racing. It looks more real.

3. The school installed a wheelchair _____ next to the stairs for the students with disabilities.

4. The new pilot had difficulty landing the plane and he had a very bumpy _____.

5. The plane _____ the runway and had to circle back.

6. The shooter didn't aim high enough and _____ his target by two metres.

7. It is very important to check your building's _____ on a regular basis so that they are ready when there is a fire.

8. When you are angry, scared, or excited, your body produces a chemical called _____.

9. The detective asked the _____ if he had finished his report.

10. Nobody survived. All the passengers and the _____ died in the plane crash.

11. He lost control and his car _____ into a tree.

12. Why are you limping? Did you _____ an ankle?

13. The doctor put his broken arm in a _____.

14. A good teacher knows how to _____ students to work with more passion.

15. His eyes were red and _____ from crying.

Warm-Up Questions

1. Have you ever participated in, or watched, a car or motorcycle race? If yes, what do you think makes these races interesting?
2. What do you think a stuntman does? Why would somebody be interested in such a job?

Comprehension

Exercise A

Watch the clip once and decide whether the following statements are true (T) or false (F). Also correct the false statements.

1.	Ken Carter, the driver, is from Nova Scotia.	T	F
2.	The event is happening in Nova Scotia.	T	F
3.	Ken is happy because a lot of people showed up for the event.	T	F
4.	It is eight in the morning when Ken arrives at the speedway.	T	F
5.	He is going to jump over 16 cars.	T	F
6.	There are two hours of stock-car racing before the jump.	T	F
7.	Ken asks the crew to prepare fire extinguishers before he starts the jump.	T	F
8.	According to Ken the crowds come to see him get hurt.	T	F
9.	If the driver is two inches off on the ramp, he will be several feet off on touchdown.	T	F
10.	Ken breaks his ankle in the accident.	T	F

Exercise B

Watch the clip one more time and answer the following questions.

1. What does each of the following spectators say about the event?
   - the man with the beard
   - the bald man with glasses
   - the man with the straw hat

2. Who is Ken's last-minute guest tonight?

3. How many feet is Ken going to jump?

4. What does Ken ask his assistants to tell the audience right after the crash?

5. What does he smell immediately after the crash? What danger is he worried about?

6. What does he promise people on the microphone after the crash?

Discussion

1. Do you think Ken chose this job because of money? What are your reasons?

2. Immediately after the crash, Ken thinks about the audience. He asks them not to leave and when he is taken out of the car he is in shock. His hands are shaking when he is holding the microphone, but he tells people that he is alright and he will be back the next night. Why do you think he cares so much about the audience? What does that tell us about the kind of man he is?

Idiomatic and Fixed Expressions

Watch the film *The Mad Canadian*, listening specifically for the following expressions. Can you guess their meaning from the context?

Expression	Definition
To make it	
To be short in something	
To turn out	
On behalf of somebody	
A hell of something	
To be kidding somebody	
To be off	

Now check your dictionary to see if you guessed right.

Writing

Imagine you are visiting Nova Scotia and you go to the speedway to watch Ken Carter perform.

You have a weblog and you have promised your readers that, using your cellphone, you will post a live update of the events. Write the updates using the present tense as if everything is happening in front of your eyes.

Example:

> 7:30 PM Hundreds of people are waiting for the Mad Canadian to arrive. They are very excited.
>
> 8:00 PM Ken Carter and his assistant are approaching the speedway in a grey car.
>
> 8:05 PM Ken is getting out of the car. He is wearing a red shirt and a white suit.

Reading

Warm-Up Questions

1. Are there any differences between the way children and adults learn languages? What are they?
2. What personality types do you think are more successful in language learning?

Vocabulary

Replace the bolded words with one of the words from the list. Check your dictionary if necessary.

chances are	frustrated
ego	self-conscious
fluently	self-esteem

1. I don't think you can use her cottage free of charge, but it is possible that she won't charge you as much as the others. _____

2. He has the biggest self-image I have ever seen. He thinks he is smarter than Einstein.

   _____

3. She is very good with languages. She speaks four languages without difficulty and is learning a fifth one. _____

4. Don't criticize yourself so much and try to build your self-worth. _____

5. He has become very insecure after he got that big scar on his face after the accident.

   _____

6. I'm not good at video games. I get discouraged too easily. _____

Taking Risks and Learning Languages

Are you a social risk taker? If you are, chances are that you are a more successful language learner as well. Research has shown that risk taking is one of the most important characteristics of successful second-language learning.

Look at the way children learn languages. They take the risk of being wrong, make guesses about language, and learn from their mistakes. Since they do not have a strong sense of ego yet, they don't care much if they are laughed at. Very often, they laugh along with others and enjoy the whole learning experience.

Learning languages is a totally different story in adults, though. They develop a language ego, a link between their language, their identity, and their self-esteem. As adults they have a strong language ego and are very comfortable in their first language. Then they start learning a second language that they don't speak fluently. They make grammatical mistakes and sometimes pronounce words in funny ways. They pause to remember words and may use the wrong word. They feel they do not seem as intelligent or as friendly as in their first language. This makes them very frustrated.

Under these conditions, self-conscious students often sit at the back of the classroom. They become shy and try to speak less because they fear they might make mistakes and appear foolish to others. When they have to speak, they try to use simple language that they are sure is correct and safe. On the other hand, risk takers continue to make guesses and use their limited second language even though they make mistakes.

In conclusion, those who take calculated risks are more successful in learning languages than those who are too careful. We learn through our mistakes and it is very important to focus on learning from the mistakes rather than focusing on what others might think of us.

Comprehension

1. According to the passage, why are children better language learners?

2. What is language ego?

3. What are some of the signs of a self-conscious language learner?

4. What are some of the signs of a risk-taking language learner?

Language Ego Questionnaire

Are you a risk taker (strong language ego) or a self-conscious learner (weak language ego)? Answer the following questionnaire to find out:

Circle the number that best describes you. Circle only one number for each item. Use the following scale:

1 The sentence on the left describes you well.

2 The sentence on the left somewhat describes you.

3 The sentence on the right somewhat describes you.

4 The sentence on the right describes you well.

Example:

I don't care if people laugh at me. 1 ②3 4 I get very upset if people laugh at me.

Number 2 has been circled. This means that this person generally doesn't mind if people laugh at him or her.

1. I don't want to make mistakes because people will laugh at me.	1 2 3 4	Everyone makes mistakes, so it's okay to try out my English.
2. I must speak perfectly or no one will understand me.	1 2 3 4	Other people will not care if I make mistakes.
3. If my English is bad, I feel very stupid.	1 2 3 4	If my English is bad, I still have strong confidence in myself.
4. Classmates who speak English better than I do really bother me.	1 2 3 4	Classmates who are better than I am don't bother me.
5. A bad score on a test means that I am not intelligent.	1 2 3 4	A bad score on a test means that I need to study harder next time.
6. When my teacher corrects me, I feel ashamed.	1 2 3 4	When my teacher corrects me, I don't feel ashamed.
7. I hate making a fool of myself.	1 2 3 4	I don't mind making a fool of myself.

Add up the numbers you circled. You should get a score between 7 and 28.

Score: _____

Score Interpretation:

7–13 Weak language ego

14–21 Moderate language ego

22–28 Strong language ego

How did you score? If you have a weak or moderate language ego, you like to be safe when you use English. You like to be certain that what you are saying is correct. But research has shown that the most successful language learners take risks. They make guesses. They try out new things. They talk with others freely. How can you become more of a risk taker?

Listening

Vocabulary

Avalanche	A mass of snow, ice, and rock that falls down the side of a mountain
Grief	A feeling of great sadness, especially when somebody dies
Appropriately	Correctly; in an acceptable way
Assess	To make a judgement about the nature or quality of somebody/something
Moratorium	A temporary stopping of an activity, especially by official agreement
Restrict	To stop somebody/something from moving or acting freely; to limit

Warm-Up Questions

1. What is backcountry skiing?
2. What is the biggest risk that a backcountry skier might face?

Avalanches: The Debate over Backcountry Skiing

Exercise A

Listen to the program and answer the following questions.
Choose the best answer.

1. What is the program mainly about?
    a) the dangers of backcountry skiing for young people
    b) how an avalanche forms, when it usually happens, and how to predict it
    c) why the young people died and how to reduce the risk of such accidents in the future
    d) the role of proper training in escaping the dangers of backcountry skiing

2. How many people died in the last accident?
    a) 4   b) 7   c) 13   d) 15

3. Where did the recent accident happen?
    a) Revelstoke, BC   b) East Vancouver, BC   c) Victoria, BC   d) Okotoks, AB

4. On average, how many people usually die each year as a result of avalanches in Canada?
    a) 4   b) 7   c) 13   d) 15

Exercise B

Decide whether the following statements are true (T) or false (F). Also correct the false statements.

1.	The skiers were inexperienced and caused the avalanche.	T	F
2.	Critics say the Canadian Avalanche Association isn't giving enough avalanche updates.	T	F
3.	The avalanche bulletin is currently issued three times a week.	T	F
4.	A Vancouver MP wants a moratorium on backcountry skiing in the area.	T	F
5.	The young man who died in Chamonix, France was a very experienced skier.	T	F
6.	The young man started skiing when he was seven years old.	T	F
7.	The young man's mother never worried about him.	T	F
8.	The young man's mother never discouraged him.	T	F
9.	The young man's mother founded a group called Parents of Lost Children.	T	F
10.	The young man's mother thinks the moratorium is not a good idea and is not practical.	T	F

Exercise C

Listen to the program one more time and identify the following people. The first one has been done for you as an example.

Name	Identity
Marissa Staddon	*One of the students who died in the avalanche*
Gord Kettyle	
Carl Staddon	
Libby Davies	
Beth Stewart	
Trevor Peterson	

Speaking

Adverbs of Frequency (Simple Present)

Exercise A

Work in teams of two. One person asks questions using the cue words. The second person answers using adverbs of frequency and explains more about the answer. Then they switch roles.

always	sometimes	seldom	almost never
almost always	frequently	rarely	hardly ever
usually	generally	never	
often	occasionally		

Example:

1. How often/forget new vocabulary?

   Student A: How often <u>do</u> you forget new vocabulary?

   Student B: I <u>usually</u> forget new vocabulary when I don't use the new words, but I <u>often</u> remember the new words if I write them down in my notebook and use them in speaking or writing.

2. How often / read a book for pleasure?
3. How often / watch a movie with subtitles?
4. How often / use a monolingual dictionary?
5. How often / speak English outside the classroom?
6. How often / your English teacher speak too fast?
7. How often / give presentations in English?

Facing Your Fear (Present Progressive)

Exercise B

Find something that you have been scared of doing. Now close your eyes and imagine yourself doing it. As you are imagining the action, describe every step to your classmate. Now switch roles and listen to your classmate describe his or her actions.

Example:

Sky diving

I am climbing the stairs and entering the airplane. Now I am inside the plane. My coach and four other sky divers are on the plane, too. The coach is holding a parachute in his hands and is explaining . . .

Canadian Outlook

Adventure in Canada

If you are a fan of extreme sports or adventure travel, there are several world-class spots across Canada where you can test your courage and get your adrenaline rush.

Here are some suggestions:

Bungee Jumping
(Ottawa River, ON)

The bungee tower on the Ottawa River in Morrison's Quarry, Wakefield, Quebec (30 minutes from Ottawa) is one of the top-10 bungee spots in the world and the highest jump in North America (60 metres, or 200 feet, above water). You could also do whitewater rafting nearby.

Zip Trekking
(Whistler, BC)

Whistler is the site of the first zip trek in the world. This is a three-hour ride hanging from a high wire by a harness and zipping at speeds of up to 80 kilometres an hour between trees and treetops and over the waters of Fitzsimmons Creek.

Tobogganing
(Les Glissades de la Terrasse, Quebec City, QC)

Zoom downhill on a toboggan at speeds of up to 100 kilometres per hour.

Driving on Frozen Water
(Mackenzie River Ice Road, NT)

This is probably the slipperiest road you will ever drive on.

Ice Climbing on Frozen Waterfalls
(Canadian Rockies around Canmore, AB)

Canmore is a small town about 100 kilometres north of Calgary. There are several frozen waterfalls in the area that are suitable for climbing any time from November to April.

Kayaking around Killer Whales
(Inside Passage, BC)

The Inside Passage runs between mainland British Columbia and the eastern side of Vancouver Island. The orcas (killer whales) come to the area to find and eat salmon.

Heli-Hiking to a Via Ferrata
(Banff, AB)

A helicopter takes you high into the mountains where you can hike and climb the mountains using metal ladders (via ferrata).

Bathtub Racing
(Nanaimo, BC)

Take part in the oldest and fastest bathtub race in the world. The bathtub is actually mounted on a superfast speedboat.

Discussion

1. If you could participate in only one of the adventures described on page 17, which one would you choose? Why?
2. Are there any other adventure sports in Canada that you know of that are not mentioned in the brochure?
3. What are some of the famous extreme sports in your place or country of origin?

Writing

Risk Profile

Exercise

Work in teams of two. Interview your classmate about the kind of person he or she is in terms of risk tolerance and fill out the form below. Then let your classmate interview you.

Name:		
Age:		
Nationality:		
Program of Study:		
Overall Risk Level (conservative / moderate / aggressive):		
Type of Risk	Risk Level (conservative / moderate / aggressive)	Example of Usual Risks
Physical risk	C M A	
Intellectual risk	C M A	
Financial risk	C M A	
Emotional risk	C M A	
Social risk	C M A	
Other information		

After the interview write a short passage about your classmate and his or her risk profile based on your interview. Try to use the simple present tense and frequency adverbs.

Here is the beginning of a sample paragraph:

> Dariya is a 19-year-old woman from Ukraine. She wants to study acting at UBC after she finishes the ESL program. Overall, she considers herself a moderate risk taker. However, there are several types of risk she seldom takes.
>
> She is a very aggressive social risk taker. She is always comfortable around people; she starts conversations easily even with people she doesn't know at all. She is an actress, so she can easily speak in front of a big audience and make them laugh and cry. She is also very good with emotional risks. She . . .

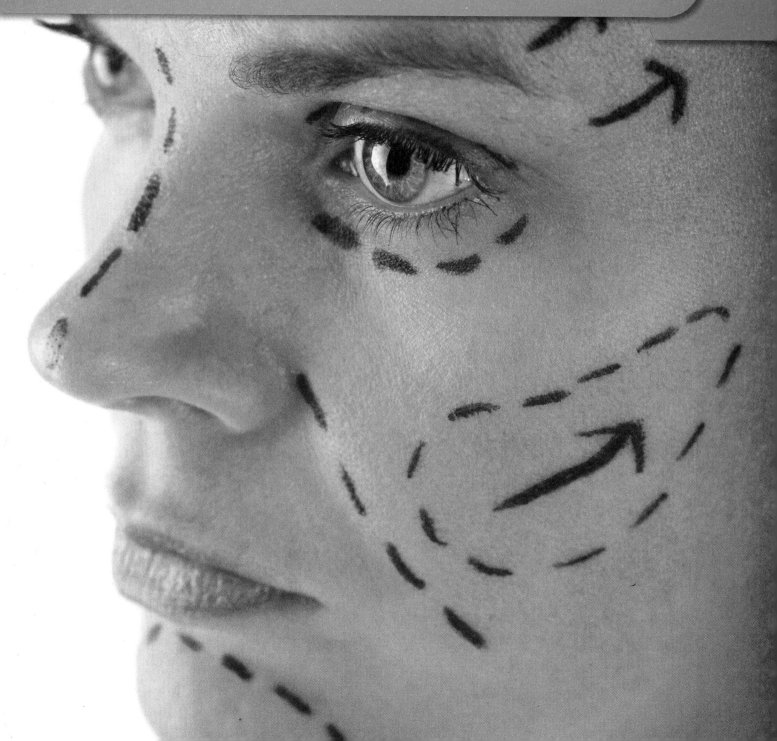

Chapter 2

STUDIO

Flawed

Introduction

Food Categories

Exercise A

The following list includes foods from different categories. In teams of two or three, put each food under the correct category in the table below. Guess first, and then check your dictionaries for the definitions of the words you do not know.

celery	cauliflower	kefir	crab	sage
haddock	kiwi	quinoa	veal	salmon
barley	whey	squash	scallops	clams
thyme	mutton	kidney	parsley	chives
yogurt	avocado	oats	steak	wheat
broccoli	herring	blackberry	trout	
lobster	peach	cheddar		

Vegetable	Fruit	Meat	Fish

Seafood	Herb	Grain	Dairy

Exercise B

Now look at the pictures below and write the word from exercise A that corresponds to each picture.

1. _____

2. _____

3. _____

4. _____

5. _____

6. _____

7. _____

8. _____

Reading

Warm-Up Questions

1. What does the word *nutrition* mean?
2. What kinds of food are not nutritious?
3. Do you think you have proper or poor nutrition? Why?

Vocabulary

Exercise A

Write each of the verbs in the box beside its corresponding definition.

stir-fry	deep-fry	roast	bake	poach	steam

_____ to cook food such as bread or cake in an oven without extra fat or liquid

_____ to cook an egg gently in nearly boiling water after removing its shell

_____ to cook food in oil that covers it completely

_____ to cook thin strips of vegetables or meat quickly in very hot oil

_____ to cook food, especially meat, without liquid in an oven or over a fire

_____ to place food over boiling water so that it cooks in the steam

Exercise B

Fill in the blanks with the appropriate words from the box below. Check your dictionary if needed.

quenched	trimmed	fortified	skimmed

1. I have high cholesterol, so my doctor recommended that I drink _____ milk.

2. My children need lots of vitamins, so I give them _____ milk.

3. I buy packaged meat with all the fat _____.

4. I can sleep only after my thirst is _____ and my hunger is satisfied.

Canada's Food Guide

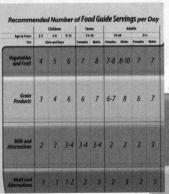

Recommended Number of Food Guide Servings per Day

| Age in Years | | Children | | Teens | | Adults | | | |
| Sex | 2-3 | 4-8 | 9-13 | 14-18 | | 19-50 | | 51+ | |
		Girls and Boys		Females	Males	Females	Males	Females	Males
Vegetables and Fruit	4	5	6	7	8	7-8	8-10	7	7
Grain Products	3	4	6	6	7	6-7	8	6	7
Milk and Alternatives	2	2	3-4	3-4	3-4	2	2	3	3
Meat and Alternatives	1	1	1-2	2	3	2	3	2	3

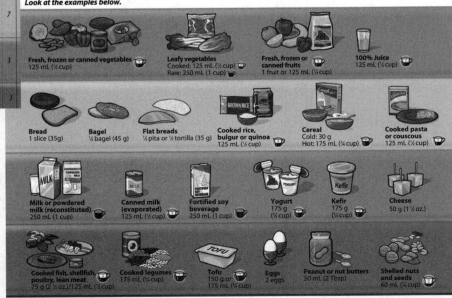

Eat at least one dark green and one orange vegetable each day.
* Go for dark green vegetables such as broccoli, romaine lettuce, and spinach.
* Go for orange vegetables such as carrots, sweet potatoes, and winter squash.

Choose vegetables and fruit prepared with little or no added fat, sugar, or salt.
* Enjoy vegetables steamed, baked, or stir-fried instead of deep-fried.

Have vegetables and fruit more often than juice.

Make at least half of your grain products whole grain each day.
* Eat a variety of whole grains such as barley, brown rice, oats, quinoa, and wild rice.
* Enjoy whole-grain breads, oatmeal or whole wheat pasta.

Choose grain products that are low in fat, sugar, or salt.
* Compare the nutrition-facts table on labels to make wise choices.
* Enjoy the true taste of grain products. When adding sauces or spreads, use small amounts.

Drink skim, 1, or 2 percent milk each day.
* Have 500 millilitres (2 cups) of milk every day for adequate vitamin D.

Drink fortified-soy beverages if you do not drink milk.
Select low-fat milk alternatives.
* Compare the nutrition-facts table on yogurts and cheeses to make wise choices.

Have meat alternatives such as beans, lentils, and tofu often.
Eat at least two *Canada's Food Guide* servings of fish each week.
* Choose fish such as char, herring, mackerel, salmon, sardines, and trout.

Select lean meat and alternatives prepared with little or no added fat or salt.
* Trim the visible fat from meats. Remove the skin on poultry.
* Use cooking methods such as roasting, baking, or poaching that require little or no added fat.
* If you eat luncheon meats, sausages, or packaged meats, choose those low in salt (sodium) and fat.

Satisfy your thirst with water!
* Drink water regularly. It's a calorie-free way to quench your thirst. Drink more water in hot weather or when you are very active.

Be active
* Being active every day is a step toward better health and a healthy body weight.
* *Canada's Physical Activity Guides* recommend building 30 to 60 minutes of moderate physical activity into daily life for adults and at least 90 minutes a day for children and youth. You don't have to do it all at once. Add it up in periods of at least 10 minutes at a time for adults and 5 minutes at a time for children and youth. Start slowly and build up.

Comprehension

1. Name two dark green and two orange vegetables.

   Dark green: _____ and _____
   Orange: _____ and _____

2. What type of cooking is not recommended for vegetables?

3. Name two varieties of whole grains and two foods made with whole grains.

Whole grains: _____ and _____
Whole-grain foods: _____ and _____

4. Below are the nutrition-facts labels of two brands of cereals. Based on the advice in the reading passage, which cereal is healthier?

Nutrition Facts Valeur nutritive		
Per ¾ cup (180g) / Pour ¾ tasse (180 g)		
Amount Teneur	% Daily Value % valeur quotidienne	
Calories / Calories 120		
Fat / Lipides 3 g	5%	
Saturated / Satirés 0.5 g + Trans / Trans 0 g	3 %	
Carbohydrate / Glucides 22 g	7 %	
Fibre / Fibres 1 g	4 %	
Sugars / Sucres 12 g		
Protein / Protéines 2 g	Ⓐ	

Nutrition Facts Valeur nutritive		
Per ¾ cup (180g) / Pour ¾ tasse (180 g)		
Amount Teneur	% Daily Value % valeur quotidienne	
Calories / Calories 120		
Fat / Lipides 1.5 g	2 %	
Saturated / Satirés 0 g + Trans / Trans 0 g	0 %	
Carbohydrate / Glucides 25 g	8 %	
Fibre / Fibres 2 g	8 %	
Sugars / Sucres 6 g		
Protein / Protéines 3 g	Ⓑ	

5. Which vitamin does milk give you?

6. What can you drink instead if you cannot drink milk?

7. Name two milk alternatives and two meat alternatives.

Milk Alternatives: _____ and _____
Meat Alternatives: _____ and _____

8. Name two methods to reduce the fat content in meat.

9. Name two times when you should drink more water.

10. How much physical activity do adults and children need each day?

Adults: _____
Children: _____

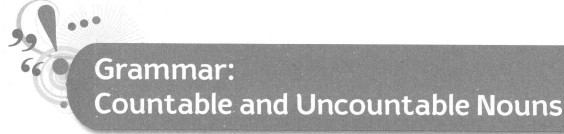

Grammar:
Countable and Uncountable Nouns

A countable noun can be singular (used with *a/an*, for example: a kiwi) or plural (for example: kiwis). An uncountable noun cannot be singular (no *a/an*, for example: don't say ~~a milk~~) or plural (no *s*, for example: don't say ~~milks~~). Uncountable nouns usually appear with *some*.

Examples:

Countable: Can I have a kiwi? Can I have two kiwis? Can I have some kiwis?

Uncountable: Can I have some milk?

Note: the word *some* can be used before uncountable nouns (some water) and before plural countable nouns (some kiwis)

You can always check nouns in a dictionary to see if they are countable (usually marked with *C*) or uncountable (marked with *U*).

Exercise A

Here's the list of some food items you saw at the beginning of this chapter. Fill in the blanks with *a/an* before countable nouns and *some* before uncountable nouns. Check your dictionary if you are not sure.

_____	celery	_____	herring	_____	trout
_____	haddock	_____	peach	_____	sage
_____	barley	_____	kefir	_____	salmon
_____	thyme	_____	quinoa	_____	clam
_____	yogurt	_____	squash	_____	wheat
_____	broccoli	_____	kidney	_____	lettuce
_____	lobster	_____	blackberry	_____	spinach
_____	cauliflower	_____	cheddar	_____	carrot
_____	kiwi	_____	crab	_____	potato
_____	whey	_____	veal	_____	rice
_____	mutton	_____	parsley	_____	pasta
_____	avocado	_____	venison	_____	sausage

Powders, gels, liquids, and gases are usually uncountable.

Examples:

laundry detergent, toothpaste, shoe polish, oil, air

Abstract nouns (ideas or non-material words) are also usually uncountable.

Examples:

advice, research, information, knowledge, love, happiness

We can use *many* before countable (plural) nouns and *much* before uncountable nouns.

Examples:

many spoons, much oil

We can use *a few* (meaning *not many*) before countable (plural) nouns and *a little* (meaning *not much*) before uncountable nouns.

Examples:

a few spoons, a little oil

Exercise B

1. Fill in the blanks in column 1 with much and many. For countable nouns, also make the noun plural.

Examples:

water → much water   book → many books

1	2		1	2	
_____	_____	information	_____	_____	plastic
_____	_____	trip	_____	_____	job
_____	_____	money	_____	_____	electricity
_____	_____	dollar	_____	_____	music
_____	_____	banana	_____	_____	song
_____	_____	apple juice	_____	_____	letter
_____	_____	butter	_____	_____	mail
_____	_____	egg	_____	_____	sand
_____	_____	sugar	_____	_____	answer
_____	_____	progress	_____	_____	luck

2. Repeat the exercise above. This time, fill in the blanks in column 2 with a little and a few. For countable nouns, also make the noun plural.

Examples:

water → a little water   book → a few books

Some words can be both countable and uncountable, but their meanings usually change. The countable word is usually a specific thing while the uncountable word is the general idea of the thing or its material.

Examples:

Give me a glass of water. (*Glass* here is a specific thing and is countable.)

This table is made of glass. (*Glass* here is the material used in making the table and is uncountable.)

I have a fish in my aquarium. (*Fish* is the live animal here and is countable.)

I had fish for lunch. (*Fish* here is the food and is uncountable.)

Exercise C

Look at the following pictures. Beside each picture put *C* if it is countable and *U* if it is uncountable. Then write two sentences with each word, one with the countable meaning and another with the uncountable meaning.

chicken

iron

tea

It is possible to make uncountable nouns countable by adding a unit to them. For example, *bread* is uncountable. We can make it countable by saying *a piece of, a slice of,* or *a loaf of bread.* (A slice of bread, two slices of bread, three slices of bread, etc.)

Some of these counting units go with specific uncountable nouns only. For example, we say

A piece of rock but a grain of sand

A flash of lightning but a clap of thunder

Exercise D

Match the units on the left with the uncountable nouns on the right.

1. _____ a leg of	a) transportation
2. _____ a bar of	b) milk
3. _____ a tube of	c) bread
4. _____ a loaf of	d) cookies
5. _____ a carton of	e) rice
6. _____ an article of	f) toothpaste
7. _____ a drop of	g) clothing
8. _____ a grain of	h) soap
9. _____ a means of	i) rain
10. _____ a package of	j) lamb

Grammar Reinforcement

Editing: Read the passage below and correct the grammatical mistakes related to articles and nouns. The first mistake is already corrected as an example. Find and correct 16 more.

We had ~~an~~ awful weather last night. There was big storm, but when I woke up, it was beautiful morning. I could hear birdsongs from my window. I went to the kitchen and looked in the fridge. I had a good luck. There were a lot of foods in the fridge. I made big breakfast for myself and the kids. I first fried egg and some sausage for Alex and I made him a glass of fresh orange juice as well. Then I prepared some oatmeals and a glass of milk for Anne. At last, I baked delicious cake for myself and had it with some coffee.

I think I will make a rice and some roasted chickens for lunch. We will then go out and have some ice creams. On the way home, we will stop at the CAA office for some advices and informations before our road trip to Halifax. We will also stop at the supermarket to buy a toothpaste, a salt, and some printing papers.

Writing

Write two paragraphs: one about the best and another about the worst food you have ever eaten. Write the name of the food, the time and the place you had it, and its ingredients as well as its taste.

The Film: *Flawed*

Video Vocabulary

The following words and expressions are used in the video. Study them before watching.

Flaw	A weakness in somebody's character or body; a problem
Romance	An exciting, usually short, relationship between two people who are in love with each other
Buck	A male rabbit, hare, or deer
Buck teeth	Top teeth that stick forward like those of a rabbit
Ugly duckling	A person or thing who at first does not seem attractive or likely to succeed, but who later becomes successful or much admired. From the title of a story by Hans Christian Andersen, in which a baby bird thinks it is an ugly young duck until it grows up into a beautiful adult swan.
Topless	(Of a woman or a girl) Not wearing any clothes on the upper part of the body, so that her breasts are exposed
Aerobics	Physical exercises intended to make the heart and lungs stronger, often done in classes, with music
Warped and off kilter	Out of shape and not in perfect balance; strange and weird
Camaraderie	A feeling of friendship and trust among people who work or spend a lot of time together
Braces	A metal device that many children (and some adults) wear inside the mouth to help their teeth grow straight
Pimples	Small, raised, red spots on the skin
Bypass	To go around or avoid something
Puberty	The period of a person's life during which his or her sexual organs develop and he or she becomes capable of having children
Nose job	A medical operation on the nose to improve its shape
To resent	To feel bitter or angry about something, especially because you feel it is unfair; to dislike
To blame	To think or say that somebody or something is responsible for something bad
Willingness	State of having no objection to doing something; state of being happy and ready to do something
To shrug	To raise your shoulders and then drop them to show that you don't know or care about something

Warm-Up Questions

1. Are you happy with your body? Is there any part of your body that you would like to change?
2. What is the difference between reconstructive and cosmetic plastic surgery?

Comprehension

Watch the film *Flawed* once and match the following questions with the answers in the box below.

1. At first, why didn't the narrator like her future boyfriend?

2. What were the three reasons she thought the relationship with her boyfriend wouldn't be successful?

3. What was the idea she found for keeping their relationship stronger?

4. What was the question she asked herself about cosmetic surgeons when she returned to Toronto from Halifax?

5. What did she realize when she looked at her old class photo on the bulletin board?

6. What changes did she go through at puberty that affected the following?
   * body
   * face
   * hair
   * teeth
   * nose

7. Who or what did she blame when she started to hate her own nose?

8. What secret did she tell her boyfriend in her postcard?

9. What happened to her when she sent the postcard?

10. What did she do at the end of the story?

11. According to her, what is the moral point of this story?

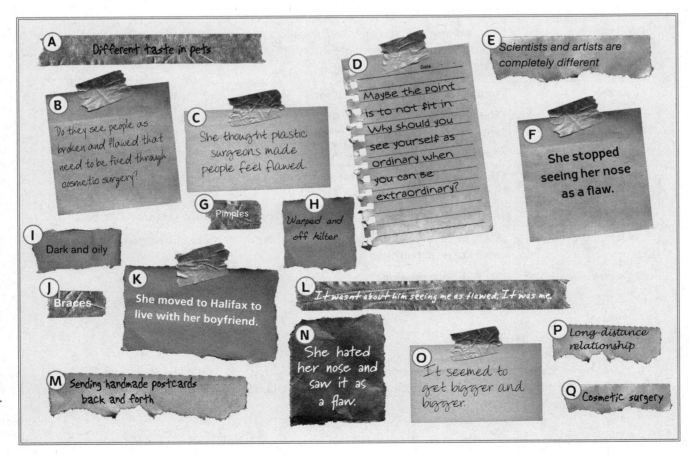

A Different taste in pets

B Do they see people as broken and flawed that need to be fixed through cosmetic surgery?

C She thought plastic surgeons made people feel flawed.

D Maybe the point is to not fit in. Why should you see yourself as ordinary when you can be extraordinary?

E *Scientists and artists are completely different*

F **She stopped seeing her nose as a flaw.**

G Pimples

H Warped and off kilter

I Dark and oily

J Braces

K She moved to Halifax to live with her boyfriend.

L *It wasn't about him seeing me as flawed. It was me.*

M Sending handmade postcards back and forth

N She hated her nose and saw it as a flaw.

O It seemed to get bigger and bigger.

P *Long-distance relationship*

Q Cosmetic surgery

Idiomatic and Fixed Expressions

Exercise A

While you watch the film, listen for the following expressions. Then try to guess each expression's meaning based on its context. The time frame is provided to help you find the expression more easily. Compare notes with your classmates and check the dictionary to make sure your guesses are right.

Expression	Frame	Definition
To write somebody off	0:45	
To work out	1:06	
To be like oil and water	1:22	
To get somebody out of one's mind	1:29	
To come up with an idea	1:33	
To keep somebody going	1:36	
To send things back and forth	1:40	
To be as good as new	2:39	
My stomach flipped	3:09	
It hit me	3:50	
It went downhill from there	5:20	
To blow somebody off	6:07	
To feel terrible for somebody	7:20	
To blame something on somebody or something else	8:30	
To let something go	9:28	
To fit in	10:48	

Exercise B

Now watch the film one last time and answer the following questions.

1. What was the narrator doing in Halifax when she met her future boyfriend?

2. What was the subject of the first postcard she sent?

3. What was the subject of the first postcard her boyfriend sent?

4. How did the man (the doctor's patient) get the nail in his fingers?

5. What was a problem with the little boy's ears?

6. What did the doctor do to the boy's ears?

7. How did the narrator get the scar between her nose and her lip?

8. What did she do for the first time when she was eight years old?

9. What did she notice when she was in grade seven?

10. How was Gracie Sullivan different from the other kids?

11. What was different about Belinda on the first day of grade eight?

12. What did her mother ask her when the narrator told her mom about Belinda?

13. What did the narrator decide to do in answer to her mom's question?

14. What did the doctor do with the second boy who had an ear problem?

Discussion

In teams of two or three, discuss the technique used in making this film. Had you ever seen something similar? Is it an effective technique for the film's message?

Reading

Vocabulary

Exercise A

Check your dictionary for the following verbs. Then fill in each blank with the appropriate verb.

binge	purge	starve
inject	shrink	strive

1. If you wash wool in hot water, it will _____.
2. You are a great student because you always work hard and _____ to do your best.
3. If the population grows any larger, there will not be enough food for everyone and lots of people will _____ to death.
4. Some people with bulimia force themselves to vomit in order to _____ their food.

5. When I'm depressed, I _____ on chocolate.
6. She is diabetic, so she had to learn how to _____ herself with insulin.

Exercise B

Choose the best synonym for each bolded word.

1. Weight loss is not usually **attainable** in a short period of time for most people.
    a) visible
    b) agreeable
    c) possible
    d) advisable

2. Do not put yourself on a harsh diet, but eat **nourishing food**.
    a) diet food
    b) nutritious food
    c) fast food
    d) junk food

3. Are you **constantly** comparing yourself with other people?
    a) completely
    b) hardly
    c) rarely
    d) regularly

4. Instead of spending money on diet pills, spend it on something **nurturing** like a massage.
    a) relaxing and useful
    b) natural and healthy
    c) expensive and classy
    d) wise and intelligent

5. You can lose weight and add muscle, but only to a certain **extent**.
    a) distance
    b) degree
    c) diet
    d) exercise

6. Think of exercise as play—your own personal **recess** or recess with friends.
    a) training
    b) free time
    c) private time
    d) busy time

Warm-Up Questions

1. What is body image? What kind of body image do you think you have?
2. What are steroids? Why do some people use steroids?

Body Image

If you had a magic wish, what would you do with it? The number one secret wish of girls eleven to seventeen is to be thinner. The body that more than half of all eleven- to seventeen-year-old boys would choose for themselves, if possible, is attainable only through steroids. Is this normal? There is nothing wrong with taking good care of your body and making it the best that it can be, and part of being a teenager is creating your identity and being very conscious about how you look. However, a huge gap exists between television and magazine images and what is normal—to the point that finding normal is not so easy. So how can you know what is normal? What should you do about the problem we all seem to be having with body image?

Understand the Human Body

The human body has limitations. For most people, looking like the latest top model is as impossible as growing six inches taller—or shrinking six inches. There is not one ideal weight for your height. Your body type, muscle mass, and bone structure have a lot to do with your family history. Yes, you can lose weight and add muscle, but only to a certain extent, and for some people even that is less attainable than for others. Also understand that weight and fitness are two separate things; in fact, muscle weighs more than fat.

Examine Your Own Body Image

Listen to how you talk to yourself about your body. Are you constantly comparing yourself with other people? Do not focus on others; focus on yourself. Strive for your own personal best, not someone else's. Do you talk negatively to yourself about your body? Do not say things to yourself that you would not dare say to your best friend because they are so mean. Be your own best friend. If you are having trouble realizing what you say to yourself about your body, try writing in a journal, reading a book about body image, or talking to someone.

Love Your Own Body

Do not think of your body as the enemy, but as something valuable that you love and take care of. Do not put yourself on a harsh diet, but eat nourishing foods. Do not think of exercise as punishment, but as play—your own personal recess or recess with friends. Instead of spending money on diet pills, diet magazines, or diet programs, spend it on something nurturing like a massage, free weights, or a great water bottle. Realize that starving, purging, or injecting harmful chemicals into yourself is as self-destructive as, if not more self-destructive than, smoking, taking illegal drugs, or binge eating. Focus on how you feel and how your clothes fit instead of how much you weigh.

Comprehension

1. What is the main message of this reading passage?

2. What is the number one wish of teenage girls?

3. What is the problem with the body that most teenage boys want?

4. Which of the following sentences is closest in meaning to the text in the box?

> There is nothing wrong with taking good care of your body . . . . However, a huge gap exists between television and magazine images and what is normal.

   a) If you take care of your body in the wrong way, you will find a huge gap between your normal body and what you see on TV or in magazines.

   b) You shouldn't take care of your body under the influence of television and magazine images.

   c) You should take care of your body, but shouldn't try to be as thin or as muscular as the models on TV or in magazines.

   d) You should take care of your body so that you can be as thin or as muscular as the models on TV or in magazines.

5. The author compares growing or shrinking six inches to what?

6. What advice does the author give to people who . . .
   - constantly compare themselves with other people?
   - talk negatively to themselves about their body?
   - have trouble realizing what they say to themselves about their body?

7. Name at least three pieces of advice that the author gives in order for you to be able to love your own body.

8. The author mentions that starving, purging, and injecting chemicals are as self-destructive as three other types of behaviour. What are they?

Listening

Vocabulary

Augmentation	An increase in the amount, value, size, etc. of something
Reduction	An act of making something less or smaller
To enhance	To increase or further improve the quality, value, or status of somebody or something
Masculine	Having the qualities or appearance considered to be typical of men
To compensate	To do something so that something bad has a smaller effect
Asset	A quality or thing that is valuable or useful to somebody
To distract	To take somebody's attention away from what they are trying to do
Insecurity	Lack of confidence in yourself
Tummy	The stomach or the area around the stomach
Consistently	Always in the same way

Warm-Up Questions

1. Is having cosmetic surgery a healthy thing to do?
2. If you had a 15-year-old child who asked your permission for a nose job, would you let him or her have the surgery? Why?

Kids' Cosmetic Surgery

Exercise A

Listen to the audio clip once. Decide whether the following statements are true (T) or false (F). Also correct the false statements.

1. Plastic surgeons in both Canada and the US are saying that their patients are getting younger.   T   F

2. Stephanie Selter is 18 years old and lives in New York City.   T   F

3. She had a nose job two years before this interview.   T   F

4. Stephanie's sister had a nose job when she was 17 years old.   T   F

5. Stephanie's sister had a nose job after Stephanie had hers.   T   F

6. Stephanie went back for more cosmetic procedures after her nose job.   T   F

7. Stephanie believes that having a procedure before you are 14 or 15 years old is not a good decision.   T   F

8. According to the American Society of Plastic Surgeons, teenagers in the United States and Canada account for about 12 percent of all the plastic surgeries performed in North America.   T   F

Exercise B

Listen to the program again and complete the following tasks.

1. Fill in the blanks (one word for each blank):
    a) Across North America, more young people are getting _____ procedures from Botox injections and nose jobs to _____ augmentation and _____ tucks.
    b) The American Society of Plastic Surgeons says that the number of teens getting cosmetic surgeries has _____ over the last _____ years and cosmetic surgeons in Canada say they are seeing a _____ phenomenon.

Answer the questions:

2. Why did Stephanie have a nose job? (Give two reasons)

3. What did Stephanie do before the surgery to hide her nose problem? (List two actions)

4. What comment did people make about Stephanie before her surgery?

5. What other procedures did Stephanie have after her nose job? (Name two)

6. Approximately how many plastic surgery procedures are done on teenagers in North America every year?
    a) 200,000
    b) 20,000
    c) 12,000
    d) 2000

7. Approximately how many cosmetic procedures are done on teenagers in North America every year?
   a) 3100
   b) 31,000
   c) 3900
   d) 39,000

Exercise C

Discuss the following questions with the rest of the class.

1. How young is too young for cosmetic surgery?
2. Is there even a place for such procedures among children? Should they be allowed?

Speaking

Countable and Uncountable Nouns

Work in teams of two to complete the following activities.

a) Packing List

It's Christmas. One of you is going on a one-week trip to Cuba and the other one is going to Moscow for the holidays. Explain what each of you is going to pack and why.

b) Grocery List

You and your roommate just got back from a long trip abroad. There is no food at home. Discuss what you need to buy. Specify how much or how many you need. You can use some of the following expressions to specify number or amount:

> *a lot of, lots of, plenty of, a little, a few, several, many, a dozen, half a dozen, a couple of, a roll*
>
> *of, a loaf of, a tube of, a package of, a bar of*, etc.

Example:

> We need a roll of toilet paper, a loaf of bread, . . .

c) Recipe

Share your favourite recipe with your partner. Specify ingredients, amounts, and cooking instructions. You can use some of the words and expressions below:

> **Numbers or amounts:** *a lot of, some, a kilo of, a pound of, a gram of, an ounce of, a pinch of,*
>
> *a litre of, a cup of, a tablespoon of*, etc.
>
> **Verbs:** *heat, cook, boil, roast, fry, bake, steam, mix, beat, crush, cut, stir, spread, add, squeeze,*
>
> *combine, melt, pour,* and *serve.*

Canadian Outlook

Check-Up on Canada's Health

Read the information below.

Total fertility rate (average number of children per woman) (2008)	1.68
Current smokers (2009)	20.1%
Infant mortality rate (per 1000 live births) (2007)	5.1
Has a doctor (2009)	84.9%
Heavy drinkers (2009)	17.2%
High blood pressure (2009)	16.9%
Life expectancy at birth—males (2005–2007)	78.3 years
Life expectancy at birth—females (2005–2007)	83.0 years
Overweight or obese adults (2009)	51.6%
Overweight or obese youth (12–17) (2009)	19.7%
Physically active (leisure time) (2009)	52.5%

What are the top three health problems for Canadians? In teams of two or three discuss if the health problems in your country or culture of origin are similar to or different from those in Canada.

Writing

Restaurant Review

Imagine you are a food critic. First, complete the sentences on page 40 with your own words. Then remove the headings and rewrite the completed sentences to form a well-organized restaurant review. Add as many sentences as you want. Try to describe the colours, smells, tastes, and ingredients.

Mangia!
Italian Restaurant
1205 Market St.
Ottawa, ON

Starters

House Salad — 6.95
Mixed greens, fresh tomatoes, scallions, and cucumber in a vinaigrette dressing

Bruschetta — 7.95
Lightly toasted bread topped with fresh tomatoes, garlic, and basil, and drizzled with extra-virgin olive oil

Minestrone Soup — 4.95
Delicious vegetable soup with beans, celery, carrots, and tomatoes

Entrées

Tuscan Steak — 22.95
8 oz. sirloin steak grilled to perfection, topped with sun-dried tomatoes, accompanied by roast potatoes and seasonal vegetables

Chicken Parmigiana — 18.95
Plump chicken breast crusted with breadcrumbs, topped with mozzarella cheese and tomato sauce, and served with linguini

Grilled Salmon — 21.95
Grilled salmon fillet seasoned with black pepper and fresh herbs, and served with fresh asparagus and mashed potatoes and parsnips

Pizza of the Day — 12.95
Freshly made thin-crust pizza. Ask your server for today's selection.

Desserts

Gelato (Ice Cream) — 4.95
Two scoops of gelato (vanilla, chocolate, or mocha flavour)

Tiramisu — 6.95
Ladyfinger biscuits dipped in coffee and layered with whipped cream, mascarpone cheese, and cocoa

Lemon Cream Tart — 5.95
Lemon cream in a pastry crust, topped with sliced almonds and powdered sugar

Beverages

House Red Wine — glass 7.95 — bottle 24.95
A full-bodied red wine from the Chianti region of Italy

House White Wine — glass 6.95 — bottle 22.95
A light, dry Pinot Grigio from northeastern Italy

Coffee & Tea — 2.75
Coffee, espresso, or choose from a variety of black and herbal teas

Pop — 1.95

Bottled Water — 7.95
1L bottle of carbonated or un-carbonated water, imported

Introduction
Last . . . (date), I decided to try . . .
The restaurant was located on . . . (address)

Greeting and Wait Time
When I arrived at the restaurant . . .

Physical Condition of the Restaurant
The restaurant was . . .
The tables were . . .
My table was . . .

The Waiter and the Menu
The menu was . . .
The waiter was . . .

The Food (Drinks, Starter, Entrée, Dessert)
I ordered a glass of . . .
It was. . .
For starters, I had a/an . . .
It was . . . , but. . .
The main dish was called . . . It was made of . . .
I had . . . for dessert. It was . . .

Price and Value
I received a bill for . . .
All in all, considering the service and the food quality, the prices were . . .

Conclusion
When I left the restaurant I felt . . .
I give this restaurant a rating of . . .

STUDIO

Chapter **3**

The Colour of Beauty

Introduction

Discrimination and Stereotypes: Self-Test

Stereotyping is the act of putting a whole group of people in a box. A stereotype is an oversimplified generalization about an entire race or group of people. Each of us is usually exposed to stereotypes from an early age, and over the course of our lives these stereotypes are repeated so many times by the people around us and the media that they become internalized and very difficult to change.

Below is a list of common racial stereotypes that you might have heard that could be misleading and hurtful to people. Can you identify the race they target? Put the name of the race in the box in front of each list. The first one has been done for you as an example.

Race	Stereotype
white (caucasian)	Golf player, self-centred
	Believes in voodoo magic, basketball player
	Good at math, terribly slow driver
	Eats shawarma, has many wives
	Materialistic and cheap, owns the media
	Eats tacos, very devout catholic

Compare your answers with a classmate and discuss the following questions.

1. Is the stereotype true about all the members of that race?
2. Are all white people self-centred? Do they all play golf?
3. Who is the most famous golf player you know? Is that person white?
4. Are there any stereotypes in your culture?
5. Do you have a lot of jokes about a certain group of people in your culture?
6. Why do you think human beings stereotype?
7. What is the problem with stereotyping?

Reading

Warm-Up Questions

1. What does the word *discrimination* mean to you?
2. Have you or someone you know ever experienced discrimination? Explain.
3. What do you think the effects of discrimination are on the victims?

Guessing Words from Context

Many authors use synonyms in their text to avoid repetition. We can use the synonyms of words in a text as clues to the meaning of the words we do not know. Circle the synonyms of the following words bolded in the passage below.

assassination	discrimination	grade

Sometimes authors use antonyms (opposites) to show contrast. Antonyms could also be used as clues to the meaning of the words we do not know. Underline the antonyms of the following words bolded in the passage below.

superior	submissive	timid	wear	decline

Blue Eyes, Brown Eyes

On April 5, 1968, following the assassination of Martin Luther King, Jane Elliott, a third-grade teacher in a small town in Iowa developed an exercise in reaction to the students' questions about the murder so that her students could personally experience the effects of prejudice and discrimination.

Elliott divided her class into two groups based on their eye colour. She made the blue-eyed students superior. She gave them extra break time, allowed them to play more popular games, gave them extra food while they were having lunch, and praised them for being more hardworking and intelligent when they were doing assignments in class. She made the brown-eyed students wear a special ribbon around their necks and drink from a separate water cooler.

Soon, the brown-eyed students became very submissive and timid. Their grades declined and they were unable to do even simple exercises that had been easy for them before. On the other hand, the grades of the blue-eyed students improved. They became bossy and bold and started to treat their brown-eyed classmates as inferiors.

After a while, Elliott told the class that she had made a mistake; in fact, it was the brown-eyed students who were superior. This time the blue-eyed students had to wear the ribbons. Almost immediately the brown-eyed students improved their marks and could easily do the lessons they had trouble with before. Now that they thought they were superior, they refused to play with the blue-eyed children.

At the end of the experiment the children were told that it was only an exercise and they were actually equal. They took off their ribbons and became friends once more.

Comprehension

1. Why did the teacher develop this exercise?

2. What advantages did she give the superior group?

3. What happened to the superior students?

4. What happened to the inferior students?

Grammar:
Simple Past and Past Progressive

Simple Past

We use the simple past tense for completed actions.

> Most English verbs take –*ed* in simple past.
>
>   walk → **walked**   talk → **talked**
>
> **If the verb already ends in *e*, just add *d*.**
>
>   live → **lived**   love → **loved**
>
> **If the verb ends with a consonant followed by *y*, change the *y* to *i* and add -*ed*.**
>
>   carry → **carried**   study → **studied** but play → **played**
>
> **If the verb ends with one vowel followed by a consonant, double the consonant when adding *ed*.**
>
>   plan → **planned**   shop → **shopped**
>
> **Irregular Verbs**
>
> The most commonly used verbs in English are usually irregular and have their own past form.
>
>   go → **went**   take → **took**   eat → **ate**
>
> **Question Form**
>
> To change simple past verbs to question form, put *did* before the subject and change the verb back to its base form.
>
>   They talked. → **Did they talk?**

Negative Form

To change simple past verbs to negative form, put *didn't* before the verb and change the verb back to its base form.

> They talked. → **They didn't talk.**

Tense Markers

The following tense markers usually come with the simple past tense: *yesterday, ago, last.*

> He left home **yesterday**.
> She died six years **ago**.
> I went to bed at 11 **last night**.

Past Progressive

We use the past progressive (also called past continuous) for an action that was in progress at a specific time in the past (sometimes not completed and interrupted by another action).

To make past progressive verbs, use the verb *to be* in the past, followed by the *-ing* form of the main verb.

> I **was writing** when he called.   We **were sleeping** when the alarm went off.

Question Form

To change past progressive verbs to question form, move *was* or *were* before the subject. Do not change the *-ing* form.

> They were talking. → **Were they talking?**

Negative Form

To change past progressive verbs to negative form, change *was* or *were* to *wasn't* or *weren't*.

> They were talking. → **They weren't talking.**

Tense Markers

The following tense markers usually come with the past progressive tense: *when, while, as.*

> **As** I was going out, a car stopped in front of our house.
> **While** I was making dinner, she called.
> I heard a noise **when** I was driving.

Exercise A

Go back to the passage "Blue Eyes, Brown Eyes" and underline all the verbs in simple past (one line) and past progressive (two lines). Then change all the verbs to negative.

Exercise B

Fill in the blanks with the correct past tense of the verbs in parentheses.

My parents ₁_____ (immigrate) to Canada from Sri Lanka when I

₂_____ (be) two years old. I ₃_____ (be) around 15 years old and

I 4_____ (shop) in a store in downtown Toronto one day when an elderly man
5_____ (look) at me angrily, 6_____ (call) me "Paki" and
7_____ (leave) the store. I 8_____ (know, negative) what to do.
I 9_____ (want) to run after him and talk to him, but instead I 10_____
(go) to the store manager and 11_____ (tell) him about the incident in his store while
I 12_____ (buy) his merchandise. He 13_____ (smile) at me and said,
"Don't take life so seriously, kid!" He 14_____ (offer, negative) to do anything to ease
my anger.

Grammar Reinforcement

Oral: Work in teams of two. Interview your partner and find out where he or she was and what he
or she was doing at the following times. Fill in the table below based on your partner's answers then
report some of the activities to the class.

Time	Place	Activity
At 8:00 AM yesterday		
At noon two days ago		
At midnight last night		
At the time your partner's child or younger brother/sister was born		
At the time of a major historical event in your partner's country or in the world (e.g., Sept. 11 attacks, when his or her favourite team won a gold-medal game, etc.)		

The Film: *The Colour of Beauty*

Video Vocabulary

All the words below are used in the fashion industry. In teams of two, go over the list to see how many of the words you have heard before. Check your dictionary for those you don't know.

top model	anorexic model	ethnic model	Amazon
Barbie	bust size	hip size	high heels
Fashion Week	casting	scouting	photo shoot
runway	consumer	demographic	aesthetics

Warm-Up Questions: Clip 1

Watch the introductory clip for this chapter.

1. What is the speaker's name?
2. What is her job?
3. Which city is she in? (Hint: look at the advertising on the taxi cabs)
4. What do you think this video is going to be about?
5. Can you guess the meaning of the following words used in this clip?

   - blatantly
   - casting
   - constantly
   - scrutiny

Check your dictionary to see if you guessed right. Then, watch the clip one more time, paying attention to the way these words are used.

Video Vocabulary for Clip 2

Replace the words in bold with their synonyms. The first one has been done as an example.
characteristics

remarkable	colour	beautiful	fight
happy	high-class	wonder	
small	viewpoint	chest	

1. Every person's face has unique features that are only found on that person. _Characteristics_

2. Renee has a very elegant face. _____

3. Renee has only a slim chance for success as a top model. _____

4. Skin pigment is still important in fashion industry. _____

5. Gucci is a prestigious designer brand. _____

6. The fashion industry has the wrong perspective when it comes to black models.

   _____

7. Renee has a bubbly personality. _____

8. Renee has worked as a model for a long time and has an impressive resumé. _____

9. Renee hopes that her campaign for getting to the Fashion Week becomes successful.

   _____

10. Renee is not worried about her bust size. _____

11. Renee wants to become an international phenomenon in the fashion world. _____

Comprehension: Clip 2

1. According to Justin, Renee's New York agent, how much will Renee make if she finally succeeds in the New York fashion market as a top model?

2. How long has Renee been in the modelling business?

3. According to the 2008 survey, what percentage of models in New York Fashion Week is white? What percentage is black?

4. According to Justin, what kinds of black girls succeed in the fashion industry?

5. Why does Norwayne (Renee's Toronto agent) think that Renee is driven and determined?

6. Why does Renee think she's like a crazy chicken?

7. How old is Renee?

8. Where was Renee born?

9. Where did she live before coming to New York?

10. When did she move to New York?

11. According to Maurilio (Fashion Week agent) what is the only problem with Renee's body?

12. What kind of black model does Maurilio's client ask for?

Video Vocabulary for Clip 3

Pay attention to the bold words in context and then match each of the words with the correct definition in the exercise that follows.

- Hiring one immigrant in a company full of Aboriginal employees is not promoting equity. It seems more like tokenism.
- As an immigrant job seeker, Kim sometimes felt she had to be flawless in order to be able to compete with others.
- Multiculturalism is an important subject in the realm of cultural studies.
- She decided to pursue a career in fashion.
- She has enlisted the services of a lawyer to help her in her fight against discrimination.
- Angelina Jolie is a renowned American actress.
- He couldn't find a job and didn't have much money left. On top of that, he soon became depressed and started drinking as a crutch.
- The government has promised to increase aid to emerging democracies in Asia and Africa.
- His answer was completely irrelevant to the question I asked.
- The young woman was killed during the political uprising that occurred after the president cheated in the election.
- We are asking people to boycott clothes from designers that use anorexic models.
- The government has tried to promote diversity by hiring visible minorities.
- I've heard you're learning Brazilian dance. Can you shake your booty like a pro now?
- Have you received your duty roster for this week?

1. ____ Tokenism	a)	Domain; area of activity; area of knowledge
2. ____ Flawless	b)	Try to do or get something; follow something
3. ____ Realm	c)	Not important
4. ____ Pursue	d)	A situation in which a group of people join together in order to fight against the people who are in power
5. ____ Enlist	e)	False support; excuse
6. ____ Renowned	f)	Developing; starting to exist or grow
7. ____ Crutch	g)	The act of doing something only in order to do what the law says or to satisfy a group of people, but not in a way that is really sincere
8. ____ Emerging	h)	Employ; hire
9. ____ Irrelevant	i)	Famous
10. ____ Uprising	j)	Bottom; the part of the body that you sit on
11. ____ Boycott	k)	Perfect; without any problems
12. ____ Diversity	l)	Ban; refuse to buy from
13. ____ Booty	m)	Multiculturalism; having a group of people from different races, cultures, and backgrounds
14. ____ Roster	n)	A list of tasks or duties

Comprehension: Clip 3

1. What expression do Lisa (*Flare* editor) and Jeanne (*Fashion TV* host) use to refer to black girls in the fashion industry? What do they mean by this expression?

2. According to Justin, why do black models have to be perfect?

3. What breaks the heart of Norwayne, Renee's Toronto agent?

4. Why does Renee want to fight hard despite all the difficulties?

5. According to Dallas Logan (fashion photographer) why don't famous designer brands want to invest in black models?

6. What does Mann (the hairstylist) think about fashion in comparison with other industries?

7. What countries are the emerging markets in the fashion industry, according to Lisa?

8. What did the editor of Italian *Vogue* magazine decide to do in reaction to the problem of racism?

9. What does Renee think the Italian *Vogue* did for the issue?

10. Why is Renee worried when she goes to model for the jean designer?

11. At the end of the film did Renee get into the New York fall Fashion Week?

Idiomatic and Fixed Expressions

Watch the full clip of *The Colour of Beauty,* listening specifically for the following expressions. Can you guess their meaning from the context?

Expression	Definition
Moment of truth	
To touch base (with somebody)	
To run around like a crazy chicken	
To break somebody's heart	
To be a sore in one's eye	
Point-blank	
To point fingers	
A nod to somebody	
To get somebody off one's back	
A beacon of hope	
Right off the bat	
To bring something to the table	

Now check your dictionary to see if you guessed right.

Writing

Leaving Feedback

A lot of video websites such as YouTube or the National Film Board of Canada allow visitors to leave comments or feedback about their videos. Here are two comments visitors left on the NFB video you just watched:

MaryRM (13 May 2010): "I absolutely hate the images in fashion magazines, the majority are what I call the heroin-addict look. The law finally had to be changed to ensure this industry doesn't keep pushing for anorexic models. The other look they like is someone without any curves. Do they wish they could dress boys? I'm not sure. I hate the idea of quota laws, but it is disgusting that they are 'looking for a white girl dipped in chocolate.' Fashion is so follower heavy, but I wonder if the women with money can pull themselves together enough to boycott any designer that does not have visible minorities. This is really disgusting even to have to think of ways to make these people change. Fashion can be fun but I intensely dislike the upper end of the fashion industry."

Olen (20 May 2010): "What is she talking about? This industry is not racist. It is a world of objects. There are no people or races to consider. There are merely amalgams of features and if they cluster in the way that the client likes, then you book the job. This industry is not about race, this industry is about who has the money and who you want to appeal to and which fantasy you want to create. She doesn't have to be a model if she doesn't want to. What a boring tired argument. It's the same one a fat girl or an ugly girl can make."

In groups of two, discuss the video and write your own short comments about the video. Feel free to talk about any aspect of the video such as the themes, music, editing, and so on.

Share your comments in class and, if you feel comfortable, post the comments online at http://blog.nfb.ca. You could ask your teacher to review the writing with you before posting it.

Reading

Warm-Up Questions

1. How many different types of discrimination can you think of? List them in your notebook and provide an example for each. The first one has been done for you as an example.

Discrimination	Example
Sexual	*a man with a job similar to a woman's gets a higher salary than the woman*
Racial	

2. Is discrimination always easy to identify?
3. Can someone discriminate without even knowing that he or she is discriminating?

Vocabulary for Case Study 1

Fill in the blanks with the words below.

consult	pair up	embarrassed
hereditary	odour	rare

1. The dance teacher _____ her students for the next dance.
2. She feels very uneasy and is _____ about being overweight.
3. The students _____ the dictionary to find the meaning of the new words.
4. A _____ disease is one that is transferred through our genes from our parents.
5. Only in the Sahara can we find such _____ animals.
6. Every time I get in his car I want to throw up because of his cigarette _____.

Case Study 1

Albert, an ESL student from France, would always sit alone and uncomfortably at the back of the class. Ms. Brown, the teacher, tried to pair him up with Melanie, another student from France, but Melanie said that she didn't want to sit next to Albert. When Ms. Brown asked why, Melanie said, "Because Albert smells like fish." Someone else said, "Yeah, he needs to take a shower." Another added, "Or maybe put on some perfume!" Some students started laughing. Albert felt very embarrassed and left the class in a hurry. The teacher became very sad, but didn't know how to react. She tried to find Albert during the break, but he had already left the school.

After class, Ms. Brown consulted with one of her more experienced colleagues who explained to Ms. Brown that Albert probably suffered from a rare hereditary disease called trimethylaminuria (TMAU), also known as fish-odour syndrome. This disorder blocks an enzyme that is responsible for breaking down smelly food compounds. Currently, there is no cure or treatment for this disorder.

Discussion

1. Is there anything Albert could do about the smell?
2. How would you react if you were Albert?
3. How would you react if you were Melanie?
4. How would you react if you were the teacher?
5. If you were in the same class with Albert, would you keep quiet about his smell or would you tell him? If you would tell him, how would you do it?

6. Do you think the school has the right to ask Albert not to attend the course because his smell is annoying to the other students?
7. Is this discrimination?

Vocabulary for Case Study 2

Rewrite the sentences below by replacing each of the words in bold with one of the antonyms in the box. Make sure to change the underlined words as well to make the sentence the exact opposite of the original.

The first one has been done for you as an example.

strict	retain	mercy	fluent
undergraduate	unreliable	solemnly	

The king showed **cruelty** toward his <u>enemies</u>.

The king showed ~~cruelty~~ (mercy) toward his <u>enemies</u>. *friends*

1. He is a very **lenient** teacher. He <u>often</u> lets us hand in homework late. _____
2. He is a **postgraduate** student. He will get his <u>master's</u> degree next year. _____
3. He **lost** his rights as the owner. They <u>will</u> take his house away. _____
4. My car is very **reliable**. It <u>never</u> breaks down. _____
5. He **happily** offered her <u>congratulations</u>. _____
6. My cousin is very **bad** in English. He speaks English <u>badly</u>. _____

Case Study 2

Professor Smith had a strict attendance policy for her undergraduate psychology class: students who missed more than five classes would be dropped from the course. The professor retained her right to excuse absences, but in her syllabus she warned students not to count on her mercy. James, a white second-year student, had already missed five classes when his unreliable Ford Escort broke down again, causing him to miss a sixth class. That same day, Li, also a second-year student, had her sixth absence as well. Li was a Chinese immigrant and the only member of her family who spoke fluent English. That day it had fallen to her, as it always did, to go with her grandmother to a doctor's appointment so she could translate. Although she tried very hard to make it back to school in time for class, the appointment ran long and Li got to campus just after class had ended.

When James called the professor to explain why he had missed class and to ask for mercy, she laughed sympathetically. She had suffered plenty of car trouble when she was a student, she told him, so she'd let him go this time—but he had better start taking the bus from now on. As the professor hung up the phone, Li knocked on her office door. Li apologized for missing class that day, promised it wouldn't happen again, and asked the professor to please give her another chance. Professor Smith shook her head solemnly and said, in a kind but sad voice, "Li, you really need to start planning better. I'm afraid I can't excuse this absence because this has happened too many times already. I'm very sorry." Li was unhappy with this response, but had expected it. She'd have to register for an extra class the next semester to make up for the credits she would lose after being dropped from this one.

Discussion

1. What is James's excuse?
2. What is Li's excuse?
3. Who has a stronger excuse? Why?
4. Why did the professor forgive James?
5. Did the professor punish Li because of her race?
6. Do you think the professor is fair to both students?
7. Is this discrimination?

Listening

Vocabulary

The following words are related to the interview. Study their definitions before listening.

Guilty	Being responsible for something bad
Innocent	Not guilty; not having done something wrong
Abolish	To officially end a law, a system, or an institution
Slavery	The state of belonging to somebody and having to work for them without pay
Fierce	Violent; angry and aggressive in a way that is frightening
Scapegoat	A person who is blamed for something bad that somebody else has done
Torture	The act of causing somebody severe pain in order to punish them or make them say or do something
Condemn	To show or suggest that somebody is guilty of something
Executioner	A public official whose job is to kill criminals

Warm-Up Questions

1. What comes to your mind when you hear the word *slavery*?
2. Do you think there was ever slavery in Canada?

Black Hands

Exercise A

Listen to the interview once and answer the following questions.

1. What is the interview about?
   a) slavery in Canada
   b) a new documentary
   c) the burning of Montreal
   d) the history of Haitian Canadians

2. Who is Tetchana Bellange?

3. Who was Marie-Joseph Angélique?

4. Why was she tortured, hanged, and burned?

Exercise B

Listen to the interview one more time and answer the following questions.

1. When was slavery abolished in Canada?

2. Who is Marcel Trudel? How did he influence Tetchana Bellange?

3. When did Montreal catch fire?

4. How much of the city was destroyed?

5. How long did Angélique's trial last?

6. Who said that she had seen Angélique committing the crime?

7. Why did Bellange enjoy playing Angélique in the play?

8. Who was Leveillé?

9. What does the film's title mean? What does it refer to? (Two things)

10. According to Bellange, why was Angélique chosen as a scapegoat? What made them choose her although there was not enough evidence?

Speaking

Asking for Clarification

Some people are not very talkative. Here are some expressions you can use to get people to explain more about something that happened in the past:

> I heard you were . . . What happened?
>
> What was it like to be . . . ?
>
> Tell me more about . . .

If the person stops in mid-story or doesn't explain enough, use these expressions to get more information:

> Wow! What happened next?
>
> What did you do then?
>
> And what happened after that?
>
> Why did you / didn't you . . . ?
>
> Did you . . . ?
>
> And what did he or she do, when you . . . ?

Exercise

Work in teams of two. One person tells a story about something that happened in the past. The second one tries to keep him or her going using the questions or statements on page 55. Here are some suggestions for topics:

Story of discrimination
Fashion mistake
Coming to Canada
Trip to . . .

Canadian Outlook

Hate Crimes in Canada

Canada is an increasingly multicultural society with people from many different ethnic, cultural, religious, and linguistic backgrounds. According to Statistics Canada, "by 2031, nearly one-half (46%) of Canadians aged 15 and over would be foreign-born, or would have at least one foreign-born parent." The number of same-sex couples will also continue to increase. With such diversity, there is always the potential for discrimination and conflicts that might even lead to hate crimes. That is why it is very important for Canadians to try to understand one another and appreciate their diversity.

Currently hate crime rates are very rare in Canada (less than 1 percent of all reported crimes). However, it is very important to see how and why hate crimes are happening.

In teams of two, try to find the answers to the following questions. Then check your answers and discuss the issues.

1. Can you number the following categories in order of hate crime frequency (from high to low)?

    ☐ Linguistic hate crimes

    ☐ Sexual-orientation hate crimes

    ☐ Racial hate crimes

    ☐ Religious hate crimes

2. Can you number the following age groups in order of being involved in hate crimes ?

    ☐ 40–75

    ☐ 25–39

    ☐ 18–24

    ☐ 12–17

3. Can you number the following victim races in order of hate-crime frequency (from high to low)?

☐ Caucasian

☐ Aboriginal

☐ Arab / West Asian (the Middle East)

☐ Black

☐ East / Southeast Asian (Japan, China, Korea, Malaysia, etc.)

☐ South Asian (India, Pakistan, Sri Lanka, etc.)

Writing

Jumbled Sentences

The following sentences tell the story of a book called *Black Like Me* by John Howard Griffin.

Exercise A

Unscramble the words in each set to make a good sentence. The first one has been done for you as an example.

1. of a book / John Howard Griffin / the title / *Black Like Me* / is / by / from Texas / a white man

   Black Like Me is the title of a book by John Howard Griffin, a white man from Texas _____ .

2. They / his / him / threatened / and / family

   _____ .

3. faced / difficulties / black / several / man / He / as a

   _____ .

4. Mexico / Texas / Griffin / move / go to / had to / from / and

   _____ .

5. southern / was / racism / In 1959 / there / a lot / in / of / United States

   _____ .

6. impossible / It / almost / was / a job / a restroom / or / to find / even

   _____ .

7. He / his / dermatologist / skin colour / the help of / changed / with / a

   _____ .

8. became / a few weeks / Griffin / hopeless / After / only / very tired / and

   _____ .

9. and / him / People / his cheques / bank clerks / to cash / insulted / refused

   _____ .

10. journey / started / then / a six-week / parts of / He / as a Negro / the Deep South / through

    _____ .

11. many other people / of Griffin's book / similar experiments / Under the influence / conducted

    _____ .

12. to experience / to change / Griffin / the South / life / as a black man / his skin colour / decided / in

    _____ .

13. and published / many white people / the report of / he came back home / When / became angry / his journey

    _____ .

14. a Turkish worker / a German journalist / For example / in 1985 / named Günter Wallraff / with racism / posed as / in Germany / their troubles / to experience

    _____ .

Exercise B

Reorganize the sentences you wrote in Exercise A to make a good paragraph. Write the full paragraph below. The first one has been done for you as an example.

Black Like Me is the title of a book by John Howard Griffin, a white man from Texas. _____

_____

_____

_____

_____

_____

_____

_____

_____

Chapter **4**

The Necktie

Introduction

What's on Your Bucket List?

In the Hollywood movie *The Bucket List*, two cancer patients (played by Jack Nicholson and Morgan Freeman) decide to fulfill their dreams and passions before they die. They make a bucket list, a list of the things they want to do before they die (or "kick the bucket"), and they start doing them one by one.

What are some of the things you want to do before you die? Make a bucket list with at least 10 items that you are really passionate about and want to do even if they seem crazy and not possible for you to do now. Share your list with your classmates, if you feel comfortable.

1.

2.

3.

4.

5.

6.

7.

8.

9.

10.

Reading

Warm-Up Questions

1. What is the best job in the world for you?
2. What salary do you think you should get for your dream job?

Vocabulary

Match each word on the left with its definition on the right.

1. _____ Contest	a) Taking or needing a lot of time
2. _____ Caretaker	b) A person who collects money for charity
3. _____ Exotic	c) Start an activity, make something available to the public for the first time
4. _____ Fundraiser	
5. _____ Launch	d) Wonderful
6. _____ Magnificent	e) A person hired to take care of somebody's property
7. _____ Promote	f) Competition
8. _____ Snorkel	g) From or in another country
9. _____ Time consuming	h) To make a product popular by advertising for it
	i) Swim underwater while breathing through a tube

The Best Job in the World

In January 2009, Tourism Queensland launched a contest to find a caretaker for Hamilton Island. The responsibilities for the job included relaxing, swimming, exploring the islands of the Great Barrier Reef in Queensland, Australia, and reporting back to Tourism Queensland and the world through blogs, a photo diary, video updates, and interviews.

The winner would be required to work only 12 hours a month for 6 months and earn a salary of AUD $150,000 (around CAD $140,000) plus access to a $4-million beachside mansion with magnificent ocean views, a private swimming pool, and a golf cart.

The news travelled fast as soon as the contest was launched and 34,684 people from 200 countries applied by posting 60-second videos explaining why they were the ideal candidate. The judges chose 15 finalists and a sixteenth applicant was chosen by popular online vote. The finalists spent four days on Hamilton Island passing through a selection process that involved interviews and a blogging-skill test as well as swimming and snorkelling tests. In the end, Ben Southall, a 34-year-old charity fundraiser from Britain was announced as the winner in a reality-TV-style ceremony. Speaking after his win, Ben said, "To go away now as the island caretaker for Tourism Queensland and the Great Barrier Reef is an extreme honour. I hope I can fill the boots as much as everybody is expecting. My swimming, hopefully, is up to standard. I look forward to all the new roles and responsibilities that the task involves."

Comprehension 1

Scan the reading passage on page 61 to find the information to complete the table below as quickly as you can.

The date the job was posted	
Job title	
Responsibilities	
Working hours	
Length of contract	
Salary	
Benefits	
Selection process	
Number of applicants	
Winner (name, age, hometown, job)	

Now read the report below on Ben's feelings about the job at the end of his contract.

The Best Job in the World: Too Good to Be True?

Mr. Ben Southall's posting as Hamilton Island's caretaker came to an end at New Year 2010. Mr. Southall now admits being a tourist ambassador for paradise was not as easy as he had thought. In fact, he had very little time for sailing, sunbathing, or relaxing and enjoying the ocean views.

He had to work seven days a week and up to 19 hours a day to **promote** the Island through events, press conferences, and official meetings.

"It has been very busy, busier than most people would have imagined, and certainly busier than I had imagined," Mr. Southall told the *Sunday Telegraph*, adding that he had been "too busy" to sit back and reflect on it all very much.

According to Tourism Queensland, Mr. Southall had visited 90 "**exotic** locations," made 47 video diaries, and given more than 250 media interviews—including a chat with Oprah Winfrey. He had also travelled the Queensland State meeting local politicians, giving speeches, and networking.

He posted more than 75,000 words in 60 separate blogs, uploaded more than 2,000 photos, and "tweeted more than 730 times," according to Peter Lawlor, Queensland Tourism Minister.

Mr. Southall admits that he is now tired out—and in need, perhaps, of a holiday.

"It was a job that needed 18 to 19 hours' work every day," he said. "Not just the interviews and the social side of it, but also sitting up late at night blogging and uploading pictures; it's very **time consuming**."

However, he still insists he enjoyed himself completely. And his bosses at Tourism Queensland are also pleased. They have actually offered him a new 18-month, six-figure contract to promote their state worldwide.

Comprehension 2

Scan the reading passage on page 62 to find the information to complete the table below as quickly as you can.

The date Ben's first contract ended	
The actual hours he worked per week	
Number of video diaries he posted	
Number of interviews he attended	
Number of trips he took	
Number of blogs he posted and the number of words he wrote	
Number of photos he posted	
Number of tweets he sent	
Length of his new contract	
His new salary	

Grammar: Adjectives and Adverbs, Comparative and Superlative Forms

The comparative form is used to compare two items. The superlative form is used to compare one part or member of the group to the rest of the group. The comparative form is almost always followed by *than* and the superlative preceded by *the*.

> British Columbia is larger <u>than</u> Manitoba. (One province compared to another province)
>
> Quebec is <u>the</u> largest province in Canada. (One province compared to all other provinces)

Adjectives

For short adjectives (one-syllable and some two-syllable adjectives), add *–er* for the comparative and *–est* for the superlative form:

> cheap → cheaper → cheapest

For long adjectives (some two-syllable adjectives and all adjectives with three syllables or more), add *more* for the comparative and *the most* for the superlative form:

> expensive → more expensive → the most expensive

For adjectives that end in *–ed*, add *more* and *the most* regardless of the number of syllables:

> tired → more tired → the most tired

Adverbs

For adverbs that end in –ly add *more* and *the most*:

quickly → more quickly → the most quickly

For adverbs that have the same form as their adjectives, follow the same rules as adjectives:

late → later → latest

Note: *good/well, bad/badly, little* and *far* have irregular forms:

good / well → better → best

As . . . as

We use the expression *as + adjective / adverb + as* to show equality:

My job is as good as yours.

I work as hard as you.

People applied as soon as they heard about the job.

We interviewed this candidate as carefully as the others.

Exercise A

Provide the comparative, superlative, and *as . . . as* forms for each of the adjectives and adverbs below.

Adjective/Adverb	Comparative Form	Superlative Form	As . . . as
far			
large			
good well			
bad badly			
little			

Exercise B

Now use the correct form from the table above to complete the following sentences. Add words where necessary.

1. My office is six kilometres from our home. My brother's office is seven kilometres from our home. My brother's office is _____ mine.
2. My room is 12 feet by 15 feet. My brother's room is also 12 by 15. His room is _____ my room.
3. I drive an SUV. My brother has an old Mini Minor, and my sister drives a sedan. I drive _____ car in the family.
4. Both my sister and I have had two accidents each. My sister drives _____ I do.
5. My brother has had no accidents at all. He seems to be _____ in the family.
6. My memory is not _____ my sister's memory. In fact my memory is even _____ my brother's. I have _____ memory in our family. I always forget things.
7. I have $2000 in my bank account; my brother has $3000. I have _____ my brother. My sister has even _____ me. She has only $1000. She has _____ amount of money in her account.

Exercise C

Fill in the blanks with the correct form of the adjectives or adverbs in parentheses. You can use simple, comparative, superlative, and equal (as . . . as) forms. Remember to add *the*, *than*, *as*, or any other words if necessary.

Examples of possible answers:

- nervous
- more nervous than
- the most nervous
- as nervous as

I worked as a contract web programmer in a small company in Calgary before I was laid off two years ago because of the recession. I tried to get a ₁_____ (new) job, but it was ₂_____ (difficult) I had thought. I had to pay my bills with my credit cards ₃_____ (soon) my Employment Insurance ran out. Day by day, my health got ₄_____ (bad). Every day, I grew ₅_____ (depressed) and ₆_____ (nervous) the day before. I ate ₇_____ (little) a child and developed ₈_____ (bad) headaches ever possible. It was ₉_____ (horrible) time of my life.

My employment counsellor, who is ₁₀_____ (helpful) person you can imagine, suggested that I go back to school ₁₁_____ (quickly) possible to upgrade my skills. I registered in a program in graphic design at a community college. The program was actually ₁₂_____ (short) web programming and it was much ₁₃_____ (easy). I found a job as a graphic designer ₁₄_____ (soon) I graduated.

I now work for ₁₅_____ (big) advertising firm in Canada. My new job is ₁₆_____ (good) my old one. It is much ₁₇_____ (interesting). Although my work hours are ₁₈_____ (long) now and I have to travel ₁₉_____ (far) from my house than in my previous job, I am ₂₀_____ (happy) now than ever before. I feel like I am working for ₂₁_____ (good) company in the world.

Grammar Reinforcement

Compare Jobs

Work in teams of two. Compare the two jobs on the next page. Each team member makes statements comparing six or seven different aspects of the two jobs. Then both members compare notes and discuss which job they think is better. Use comparative and *as . . . as* structures wherever possible.

Example:

> Job A is easier because the calls are inbound. (People call you. They need your help, so they are usually nicer.) Job B is more difficult because it involves collection. You have to call people and make them pay, so clients are normally not as nice as in Job A.

Job A	Job B
Title: Call-centre agent (bilingual–inbound)	**Title:** Call-centre agent (Jr. Collection agent)
Terms of Employment: Permanent, Part-Time, Day	**Terms of Employment:** Permanent, Full-Time, Day
Salary: $14.00 hourly for 30 hours per week	**Salary:** $24,000.00 yearly for 40 hours per week, bonus, other benefits, dental benefits, group insurance benefits
Anticipated Start Date: As soon as possible	**Anticipated Start Date:** As soon as possible
Location: Mississauga, Ontario (2 vacancies)	**Location:** Mississauga, Ontario (7 vacancies)
Education: Completion of high school	**Education:** Some high school, Completion of high school
Credentials (certificates, licences, memberships, courses, etc.): Not required	**Credentials (certificates, licences, memberships, courses, etc.):** Not required
Experience: 1 year to less than 2 years	**Experience:** Experience an asset
Languages: Speak English, Speak French, Read English, Read French, Write English, Write French	**Languages:** Speak English, Read English, Write English
Work Setting: Private sector, utilities	**Work Setting:** Private sector
Business Equipment and Computer Applications: General office equipment, Electronic mail, Spreadsheet software, Database software	**Business Equipment and Computer Applications:** General office equipment
Specific Skills: Answer inquiries and provide information to customers, Explain the type and cost of services offered, Maintain records and statistics	**Security and Safety:** Bondable
Work Conditions and Physical Capabilities: Fast-paced environment	**Work Conditions and Physical Capabilities:** Fast-paced environment, Work under pressure, Tight deadlines, Repetitive tasks, Attention to detail, Noisy
Transportation/Travel Information: Public transportation is available	**Transportation/Travel Information:** Own vehicle, Travel expenses not paid by employer, Public transportation is available
Work Location Information: Urban area	**Essential Skills:** Reading text, Oral communication, Working with others, Problem solving
Essential Skills: Oral communication, Working with others, Problem solving, Significant use of memory, Computer use	**Other Information:** We are looking for people who want a career, not a job. We are hiring immediately, therefore candidates must be able to start ASAP. Pleasant phone manners, ability to leave effective messages required.
Employer: ABC Employment Solutions (Placement Agency)	**Employer:** DEF Collection Services
Contact Name: John Smith	**Contact Name:** Jane Smith
By Email: j.smith@abc-employment.com	**By Email:** jsmith@def-collection.com

The Film: *The Necktie*

Warm-Up Questions

1. Have you ever had a job that was boring? How long did you stay in that job?
2. Have you ever had a really interesting job? How did you find that job?

Comprehension

Exercise A

Watch the film and complete the table of events below as you are watching. Use the cue words in each box to take notes about the events in that particular scene. The first one has been done as an example.

At home Early morning	*Receives mom's gifts (accordion, tie, and card) for his 25th birthday. Is very happy, excited, and energetic. First day of work for a big company.*
On the elevator At work	
In the lobby At work	
In his office Clerk with a cart	
Leaves office Paper in hand	
Back home Birthday	
Next day At work	
On the elevator Elevator buttons	
Back home Final scene	

Exercise B

Now use your notes from above and write a short summary of the film in paragraph form. Use as many adjectives as you can to describe the man's feelings.

Symbolism

Jean-François Lévesque, the writer and director of this film, has used several symbols in this film. For example the number of floors in the company building is a symbol of the years of working life. Watch the film one more time and in the table below, write what you think each of the following elements symbolizes or means in the context of the film.

Element	Meaning
The ties and their patterns/colours	
The accordion	
The name of the company	
The number of floors in the company building	*symbol of the years of the character's working life*
The frame in front of the boss's face	
The shape and colour of all the other characters	
The rain	
The plant in Valentin's house	

Can you find any other symbols in the film? What do they mean?

Interview with Jean-François Lévesque
Video Vocabulary

All the words and expressions below are related to the video you are going to watch. In teams of two, go over the list to see how many of the words and expressions you have heard before. Check your dictionary for those you don't know.

2D/3D	composite	isolate	puppet
absurdity	control freak	merge	storyboard
animatic	façade	pantomime	to shoot (a film)

Comprehension

1. How did the director get the idea for the movie *The Necktie*?

2. What was the hardest part in making the film?

3. How did he make the accordion-playing scene?

4. Why did he combine 2D hand-drawn animation with 3D puppet animation?

5. How did he combine 2D with 3D animation?

6. Valentin, the main character in the film, doesn't have a mouth or eyebrows. How did the director create emotions in the character?

7. How did the following famous directors influence Jean-François Lévesque? Write the area of influence under each name.

Tim Burton	Nick Park	Terry Gilliam

Writing

The Necktie is a silent film. If it weren't silent, what kind of conversation would happen between the characters?

Create conversations between characters for the following scenes:

* The clerk knocks and enters Valentin's office to get the documents.

* Valentin finds the clerk shredding the documents.

- Valentin goes to his boss to complain about the shredding.

Reading

Warm-Up Questions

1. What was your favourite subject at school?
2. If you have/had a job, is/was it related to your favourite subject?
3. What kind of job do you think matches your personality?

Vocabulary

Replace the bolded words with one of the words from the list. Check your dictionary if necessary.

miserable	nay	sufficiently	sensible
hence	inventory	stretch	

1. Such a job is very difficult to find, **not only so, but** nearly impossible. _____
2. They have already fired him. **Therefore**, any other threats are useless and ineffective. _____
3. She has prepared herself for the interview **enough**. _____
4. The interviews usually **continue** over several hours. _____
5. He looks very **unhappy** since he started his new job. _____
6. If you don't enjoy your job, the **logical** solution is to quit and look for a better one. _____
7. I will **make a list of** all the documents I need for my job search. _____

Read the passage below and answer the questions that follow.

When You Don't Know What Career You Want

The purpose of choosing or changing a career is to find career satisfaction, or—in a word—happiness. More than that, it is to find a career you will *love*. Work that you can't wait to get up in the morning and go do. Work that you love so much, you can't believe you are being paid to do it—since you'd be willing to do it for nothing.

Finding a career you can love depends on there being a match between what you love most to do, and what is available *out there*. For example, if some *hot* new career is available, but it involves working with paper, while you love working with people, then that career is going to make you miserable, no matter how easy it may be to find a job in that field.

Hence, it doesn't matter that a career is *hot* or *easy* to get into. What matters is that you and the career should be happy with each other, nay, be in love with each other. There are few greater joys in life than to find such a career.

As we can see from the diagram on the next page, finding such a career depends upon it matching the skills you love to use, plus your favourite subjects, the people you love to help or work with, the kind of place where you love to work, your goals and the employer's goals, and a salary that satisfies your needs.

Chief among these are the skills you love to use and your favourite subjects. While you may think you know what these are, in most cases your self-knowledge could use a little more work. A weekend would do. In a weekend, you can inventory your past sufficiently so that you have a good picture of the kind of work you would love to be doing. You can, of course, stretch the inventory over a number of weeks, maybe doing an hour or two one night a week, if you prefer. It's up to you as to just how you do it.

But it is the best way. Indeed, it is the only sensible path to career satisfaction. *Don't decide on your future before you have first inventoried your past.*

Comprehension

Exercise A

1. Which statement below best summarizes the main idea of this passage?
   a) You have to list your skills in detail in order to find your ideal job.
   b) To find a good job, you first have to research the company and the people who work there very well.
   c) An ideal job is one that is chosen based on your self-knowledge and that brings you happiness.
   d) An ideal job is one that is easy and hot and brings you a lot of money.

2. Which of the following is *not* considered an important factor in your job search?
   a) your money expectations
   b) the popularity of the job
   c) your personal interest in the field of work
   d) the company's mission

3. Which of the following is closest in meaning to the sentence in the box?

> Finding a career you can love depends on there being a match between what you love most to do, and what is available *out there*.

   a) There is not much relationship between what you love to do and what is available out there in the market.
   b) Sometimes you know what you love to do, but the job might simply not be available in the market.
   c) If the job you love to do is not available in the market, you can certainly find another one.
   d) Don't be afraid to compete in any matches out there to get the job you love to do.

Exercise B

Fill in the flower diagram below based on the instructions in the preceding passage to discover your ideal job.

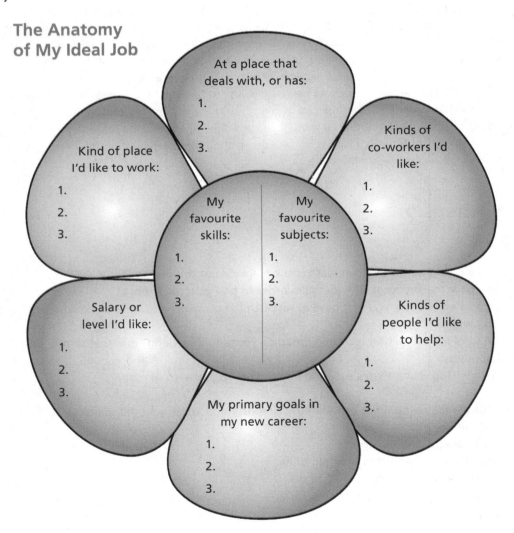

The Anatomy of My Ideal Job

At a place that deals with, or has:
1.
2.
3.

Kind of place I'd like to work:
1.
2.
3.

Kinds of co-workers I'd like:
1.
2.
3.

My favourite skills:
1.
2.
3.

My favourite subjects:
1.
2.
3.

Salary or level I'd like:
1.
2.
3.

Kinds of people I'd like to help:
1.
2.
3.

My primary goals in my new career:
1.
2.
3.

Listening

Warm-Up Questions

1. Have you ever taken an online course?
2. Do you prefer an online course or a face-to-face course? Why?

Online Job Training

Exercise A

Listen to the program and answer the following questions:

1. What is the program mainly about?
   a) online courses for Canadian job hunters
   b) online courses for immigrants in Canada
   c) online courses for future immigrants to Canada
   d) the problems of finding a job in Canada

2. Which Canadian city is currently offering the workshops?

3. What three services does the program offer?

4. What does IPSO stand for?

5. IPSO is run by ISIS. What does ISIS stand for?

6. What was Diana's job in Israel before she came to Canada?

7. When did Diana receive her Canadian licence?

8. How long are the IPSO workshops?

9. Which three countries account for one-third of all immigration to Canada?

10. What does the reporter mean by bad surprises?

Exercise B

Listen to the program one more time and identify the following people. The first one has been done for you as an example.

Name	Identity
Carmel	CBC reporter and host of the program called *Link*
Maria	
Shazia	
Robert	
Diana	

Idiomatic and Fixed Expressions

The following expressions are used frequently in the context of job searches and interviews. Which ones have you heard before? What do you think they mean?

Expression	Definition
Dead-end job	
Cold call	
Give notice	
Lay off	
Keep/stay in touch	
Get a/one's foot in the door	
Keep one's eye on the prize	

Now check your dictionary to see if you guessed right.

Speaking

Avoiding *Ums* and *Ahs*

Read the conversation below.

Why did you leave your last job?

Um, I was a . . . sales assistant and I, ah, worked at this um big grocery store. My manager was like, ah, a bit too controlling. He wanted to, you know, control us like we were his kids or something. I couldn't take it anymore. So I kind of decided to leave.

There are so many pauses and *ums* and ahs and *likes* that it is difficult to follow the speaker.

Our brain very often produces verbal pauses (such as *um*, *ah*, *oh*, and *like*) when it is searching for words or ideas. This is more frequent in people who are not native speakers of a language.

There are several gap-fillers we can use instead of *ums* and *ahs* to give our brains time to think and at the same time make our conversation seem natural.

Here are some examples:

Well, let me see . . .
That's a very good question.
Let me explain it this way . . .
Let me put it this way . . .
That's a tough question. Let me think . . .
The best way to answer your question is . . .
How can I explain this?
As a matter of fact . . .
To tell you the truth . . .

Exercise A

Pair work: In teams of two, ask and answer the following common job-interview questions. If you cannot think of an answer right away, fill the gap with an expression you learned above.

- Why do you want to work for this organization?
- Tell me about your dream job.
- What kind of person would you refuse to work with?
- What is your greatest strength?
- What is your biggest weakness?
- What has been your biggest professional disappointment?
- What kind of salary do you need?

Canadian Outlook

Canadian Work Culture

Canada is a very large country and each province or territory has its own culture or subcultures. For example, there are many differences between francophone, anglophone, and First Nation cultures in how they behave at work. There are, however, certain behaviours that are expected in most workplaces in Canada.

Discussion

As a group, use your knowledge of Canadian culture and discuss the answers to the following questions. Again, remember that there might be more than one answer to some of the questions, depending on the region.

1. How important is punctuality in the Canadian workplace? How is it different from other cultures that you know? Is it acceptable to visit people without an appointment?
2. Is it better to use titles such as Mr., Mrs., and Ms. to address your colleagues or can you use their first names?

3. When introducing your colleagues to other people, do you introduce them based on gender or rank?
4. Is it acceptable to touch another person when talking to him or her?
5. How much space do people normally need when they are face to face with somebody else?
6. Is it acceptable to kiss close colleagues or friends on the cheek? If yes, how many times?

Writing

Writing a Resumé

A resumé is a summary of your academic and work history as well as any personal characteristics that will prove to the employer that you fit in with the company. A good resumé will help you get a job interview and hopefully a good job.

Exercise A

Write a resumé for your dream job based on the ideal job exercise on page 72. You may use the template below or write your own. Bring some copies of your resumé to share with your classmates.

YOUR NAME
Address ● City, Province, Postal Code ● Phone Number ● Email address

PERSONAL PROFILE
• Academic achievements, career goals, etc.

EDUCATION
School Name—School City, Province
Degree Expected or Obtained, Degree Expected Date

School Name—School City, Province
Degree Expected or Obtained, Degree Expected Date

EXPERIENCE
Professional Experience
Company Name, Dates of Employment
• Job description, responsibilities, and accomplishments

Professional Experience
Company Name, Dates of Employment
• Job description, responsibilities, and accomplishments

Internship
Company Name, Dates of Employment
• Job description, responsibilities, and accomplishments

ACTIVITIES
List sports, clubs, etc. as well as dates of involvement

Chapter 5

Beyond Memory

Test Your Memory

How good is your memory with words? How many words can you memorize in a short period of time? There are 20 words in the left column of the table below. All the words are taken from chapters you have already studied. If you do not remember the meaning of a word, look it up before starting the exercise.

Now, study the list for a maximum of five minutes, then cover the left column and try to remember all 20 words *in the correct order* and write them in the right hand column in less than four minutes.

Crazy	
Caretaker	
Toddler	
Sunscreen	
Hip	
Exotic	
Puppet	
Canoe	
Pantomime	
Contest	
Roller coaster	
Avalanche	
Stuntman	
Slave	
Crash	
Anorexic	
Barbie	
High heels	
Runway	
Photo shoot	

Write the total number of words you remembered. TOTAL: _____
Write the total number of words you remembered in the correct order. TOTAL: _____

Did you use any techniques to memorize the words?

Go around the class and find the people with the highest marks. Ask them if they used any techniques to memorize the words and make a list of all the techniques you and your classmates used.

Reading

Warm-Up Questions

1. Do you remember the name of your teacher in the first grade?
2. Do you remember the telephone number of your best friend in the fifth grade?
3. Do you remember certain types of information more easily than others? Why?

Vocabulary

Exercise A

Check the adjectives below in a dictionary, and then fill in each blank with the appropriate adjective.

permanent	temporary	random	factual

1. More than half the workers at this factory are _____. The company won't keep them for long.
2. When I put my iPod on shuffle, it plays music in a _____ order.
3. Some men suffer from _____ hair loss. They lose their hair forever.
4. My teacher checked all the information in my essay to make sure it was correct and she found two _____ errors.

Exercise B

Check the verbs below in a dictionary, and then fill in each blank with the correct form cf the appropriate verb.

store	recall	rhyme	recognize

1. I _____ his voice as soon as I picked up the phone, but I couldn't _____ his name.
2. The words *tree* and *free* _____.
3. Today small cellphones can _____ more information than large desktop computers could 10 years ago.

Memory

Memory is the process of **storing** experiences in the brain and **recalling** them later. People use their memories during every moment of their lives. They must remember words and ideas to speak or to write. Even when walking or eating, people remember the movements they learned as children.

Scientists know that memories cause chemical changes in the neurons (nerve cells) in the brain. The chemical changes create what are called *memory paths*.

These paths can remain in the brain for seconds or for a person's entire life.

Levels of Memory

Many scientists believe that there are two levels of memory. One level is short-term memory, or working memory. The other level is long-term memory, or permanent memory.

Short-term memory is a way to store information temporarily. It lasts about 15 to 30 seconds. An example is keeping a telephone number in mind after looking it up and while dialling.

Long-term memory is the storage of information for longer periods. It can last days, months, years, or a lifetime. Repeating and practising motions or tasks help the brain to store information for a long time. If a person dials a telephone number many times, the number will move from short-term to long-term memory.

Types of Memory

Scientists also think that there are different types of memory. These include motor-skill, factual, and emotional memory.

Motor-skill memory tells people how to do physical things that they have done before. It can be short-term or long-term. People use motor-skill memory to copy a dance step and to ride a bicycle.

Factual memory is the storage of facts. It can be short-term or long-term. Factual memory lets people remember faces, numbers, and the experiences that happen to them.

Emotional memory is the memory of emotions. It is long-term. For example, people tend to remember very frightening experiences throughout their lives.

Some scientists think this happens so that people are prepared for problems in the future.

Remembering

People can pull out information stored in memory through either recall or recognition. Recall means that someone can remember something learned earlier. Recognition is the ability to identify something that has been seen or experienced before. Recognition is easier than recall. It may be easy to **recognize** a person's face, but it is more difficult to recall the person's name.

Patterns are also easier to remember than random information. For example, it is easier to remember a poem that **rhymes** than one that does not.

Forgetting

Being unable to remember things is called *forgetting*. A major reason for forgetting is the passage of time. People also tend to forget things that they do not practise or review. Sometimes a disease or an injury to the brain can cause people to forget.

In general, people do not like to forget. But forgetting serves some important purposes. The brain forgets information that it no longer needs. Then it may be open to learning new information. Forgetting can also help people to survive painful experiences.

Comprehension

1. What is the definition of *memory* according to this passage?

2. How are memory paths created?

3. How long do memory paths last?

4. What are the two memory levels? Give an example of your own for each level.

5. Name the three memory types and define each.

6. What is the difference between recognition and recall?

7. Give an example of how the brain finds patterns easier to keep.

8. Give two examples of how forgetting can be useful.

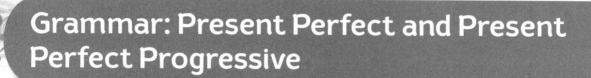

Grammar: Present Perfect and Present Perfect Progressive

Present Perfect

---

have/has + past participle of the verb

Examples:

I **have** seen that movie. He **has** talked to his parents.

Negative form: I **have not** (**haven't**) seen that movie. He **hasn't** talked to his parents.

Question form: **Have** you seen that movie? **Has** he talked to his parents?

The present perfect tense is used for two main purposes:

1. to describe actions in indefinite past
2. to describe actions that started in the past and continue to the present

1. Indefinite Past

In this sense, present perfect tells us that something happened (or didn't happen) in the past, but it is not important when it happened.

Note: When the time of the past action is mentioned, simple past tense is used.

In the table below, compare the sentences on the left (indefinite past) with those on the right (definite past). Notice the use of adverbs such as *never*, *ever*, and *already* with the indefinite past.

Indefinite Past (Present Perfect)	Definite Past (Simple Past)
I **have seen** that movie.	I **saw** that movie <u>yesterday</u>.
Have you <u>ever</u> **broken** an arm?	**Did** you **break** your arm <u>last June</u>?
I **have** <u>never</u> **visited** Paris.	I **didn't visit** Paris <u>last year</u>.
I **have** <u>already</u> **finished** my homework.	I **finished** my homework <u>an hour ago</u>.

Exercise A

Using the adverbs in parentheses, change the following sentences from definite past to indefinite past (present perfect). Remember to remove any adverbs (*ago*, *yesterday*, *last*, etc.) that refer to specific times.

Example:

> I saw that woman last week. (before) → I have seen that woman before.

1. Somebody used this cup an hour ago. (before)
2. The plane landed an hour ago. (already)
3. He sent me the results two minutes ago. (just)
4. Did you read Eileen Kernaghan's fantasy novel? (ever)
5. I didn't learn those memory tricks. (never)

2. From Past to Present

Present perfect is also used for actions or situations that started in the past which connect or continue to the present. In this sense, the adverbs *since*, *for*, and *so far* are often used.

Examples:

> I have talked to her five times so far. (from the first time I talked to her until now)
>
> I have been here since July. (I came here in July and I am still here.)
>
> I have known that guy for five years. (I saw him for the first time five years ago and I am still in contact with him.)

Note: Since is used to mark the *beginning* of the action. For is used to mark the *duration* of the action.

> I have lived here since June. (when the action started)
>
> I have lived here for five months. (how long the action has lasted)

Exercise B

Fill in each blank with *since* or *for*.

1. I have had this jacket _____ 2011.
2. I have had this jacket _____ two years.
3. We haven't stopped _____ 30 minutes.
4. We haven't stopped _____ 30 minutes ago.
5. I haven't heard from him _____ last month.
6. I haven't heard from him _____ one month.
7. She hasn't eaten _____ you left.
8. She hasn't eaten _____ a whole day.

Present Perfect Progressive

> *have/has* + *been* + present participle of the verb (v + -*ing*)
>
> Examples:
>
> I have been going there for a long time.
> She has been talking for two hours.
>
> Negative form:
> I have not (haven't) been going there for a long time.
> She hasn't been talking for long.
>
> Question form:
> Have you been going there for a long time?
> Has she been talking for long?

The present perfect progressive tense is used to express an activity or situation that has been in progress from the past to the present. The present perfect progressive is very similar to the second use of the present perfect on page 82 with the difference that the action can be interrupted in present perfect while in present perfect progressive the action is continuous.

Look at these examples:

I have gone there three times since July.

I have been going there since July.

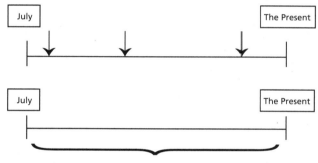

Exercise C

Use the simple present, present perfect, or present perfect progressive tense of the verbs in parentheses to complete the following sentences.

Recently, my mother ₁ _____ (act) strangely. She ₂ _____ (lose) her way home several times in the past month and she ₃ _____ (confuse) my name with my brother's. I am worried about her. I think she might have Alzheimer's disease. At the moment, I am sitting in my room looking out the window. It ₄ _____ (rain) non-stop for two hours now. I ₅ _____ (finish) reading a book about the disease. I ₆ _____ (think) about the subject all week. It seems like although the scientists ₇ _____ (try) to find a cure for the disease, there ₈ _____ (not, be) much progress.

Canadian scientists ₉ _____ (discover) a particular gene called p73 that ₁₀ _____ (protect) the brain as people age. To prove this theory, Dr. Kaplan, the head of the team ₁₁ _____ (begin) collecting DNA samples from people with Alzheimer's and those without the disease to compare the number of p73 copies in the two groups. The results will be published soon.

It ₁₂ _____ (be) very satisfying to receive thousands of letters telling me how much my techniques ₁₃ _____ (help) people with specific memory problems. I am grateful that you ₁₄ _____ (give) me the opportunity to contribute in this way. For many years I ₁₅ _____ (lead) workshops on memory management all over the world, and I ₁₆ _____ (write) other books. This book helped me find my path in life, just as it ₁₇ _____ (help) others. The time ₁₈ _____ (come) for a revised edition. I ₁₉ _____ (make) very few changes, simply clarifying certain concepts. I'd like to thank all my teachers who ₂₀ _____ (contribute) so much to my life and happiness. Some of you I ₂₁ _____ (know) as gurus, some I ₂₂ _____ (know) as personal friends, and others of you ₂₃ _____ (come) to me in the form of books. To all of you I ₂₄ _____ (send) my love and deep appreciation.

Grammar Reinforcement

Work in teams of two. Student A makes a grammatically correct question with the words in each set below by adding prepositions, auxiliaries, articles, and correct verb tenses. Student B answers. Student A writes down student B's answers to present to class. Then they switch roles.

Example:

> How many times / you / try to pass / test / until now?
>
> Student A: How many times **have** you **tried** to pass **the** test until now?
>
> Student B: I have tried it two times until now.
>
> Student A (reports): He (or She) has tried to pass the test two times until now.

1. you / ever / wish / you / be / someone else?
2. How long / you / be / study / this school?
3. you / be / listen / my questions?
4. How many novels / you / read / your life?
5. Which cities / you / visit / since / you / come / this country?

The Film: *Beyond Memory*

Video Vocabulary

The following words and expressions are used in the video. Study them before watching.

Dementia	A serious mental disorder caused by brain disease or injury that affects the ability to think, remember, and behave normally
Diagnosis	The act of discovering or identifying the exact cause of an illness or a problem
Neurologist	A doctor who studies and treats diseases of the nerves
Cognitive	Connected with mental processes of understanding
Neural imaging	Taking a picture of the brain using different methods such as CAT scan or MRI

Pathology	The scientific study of diseases and causes of death
Gerontologist	A person who studies the process of people growing old
Neurodegenerative disease	A disease that progressively destroys nervous tissues and functions
Assessment	The act of judging or forming an opinion about somebody or something; for example about the condition of a disease and the needs of the patient
Aggravate	To get or to make something worse
Sensation	The ability to feel through your sense of touch
Intricate	Having a lot of different parts and small details that fit together; complex
Avid	Very enthusiastic about something (often a hobby); passionate
Disrupt	To make it difficult for something to continue in the normal way

Warm-Up Questions

1. Have you ever met anyone with dementia?
2. What problems do you think a person with dementia would have? How would his or her life be different from others?

Exercise A

Watch the first part of the clip and provide the following information:

1. Elaine's full name.
2. The name of her disease.
3. Her current age.
4. Number of children.
5. Who she lives with.
6. The date when she was diagnosed.
7. Her age when she was diagnosed.
8. The name of the company she worked for.
9. Her job at that company.
10. The name of the university she was referred to by her neurologist.

Exercise B

Now watch the clip a second time and answer the following questions.

1. Why does Elaine need a logbook?

2. What kind of problem does she have with knitting?

3. Why can't she read books (novels)?

4. What kind of material does she read these days?

Exercise C

Watch the second part of the clip and answer the following questions.

1. Which of the following is not part of the normal clinical diagnosis of Alzheimer's?
   a) taking the patient's history
   b) a blood test
   c) a neurological examination
   d) an assessment of cognitive functions
   e) neural imaging

2. In the picture below identify the neurofibrillary tangle and the senile plaque, then match each term with its definition.

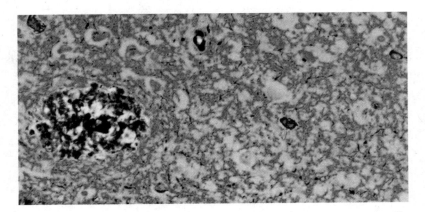

    a) Normal proteins break apart and their fragments stick together and break the electrical signals in the brain. This is the definition of a _____ .

    b) Structures that transfer nutrients between cells are changed and cells collapse and die. This is the definition of a _____ .

3. In the picture below identify the normal brain and the brain with dementia.

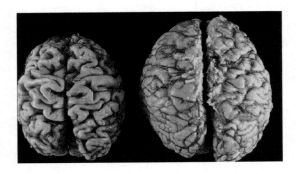

4. In Elaine's cognitive assessment session with Dr. Claudia Jacova, Elaine was asked to do four things. What were those? (The first one has been done for you as an example)

1. *remember the date*	2.
3.	4.

5. Which of the four tasks above was Elaine unable to complete?

6. Name two of the things a doctor usually looks for during the neurological exam.

7. What is the current cure for Alzheimer's?

8. What kind of patients receive the most benefit from medication?

9. Lynn Jackson, Elaine's friend, also suffers from dementia. What do Lynn and Elaine discuss at the end of the clip?

Writing

Childhood amnesia is the term that describes the inability of most adults to remember the time they were very young. Scientists believe the average age for our earliest memory is three years and six months. When you think about your childhood, what is your earliest memory? In a paragraph or two, write about your earliest childhood memory. Describe what you remember. Why do you think you still remember that particular event or episode?

Reading

Warm-Up Questions

1. What is visualization?
2. What is association?
3. Have you ever used visualization and association as memory tricks?

Memory Training

Have you ever felt embarrassed because you forgot the name of a colleague or a friend? Have you ever lost marks because you forgot the answers to some questions on a test? Have you ever memorized new words only to find that a week later you couldn't recall most of them? Don't worry! Training your memory is not a difficult task at all.

Since ancient times, humans have tried to understand how memory works and to find ways to improve their memory. A powerful memory was especially important to our ancestors as they did not have access to devices like handheld computers or cellphones to carry all their information around. Ancient Greeks devised several methods for memory improvement most of which we still use to-day. However, the science behind memory training has made great progress since ancient times and cognitive scientists and psychologists have learned a lot more about human brain and memory. These scientific findings and the practical wisdom of our ancestors form the basis for most modern memory training techniques.

Let's look at some of these techniques.

Take a couple of minutes to memorize the number below:

612192733404854

Now write it from memory in the box below:

Was it easy? How long do you think you can retain the number in memory? Will you remember it tomorrow? What if you knew that there is a mathematical relationship between these digits? Would it make it easier?

Look at the same digits grouped differently:

(6) (12) (19) (27) (33) (40) (48) (54)

Have you found the relationship?

(6) + 6 = (12) + 7= (19) +8 = (27) +6 = (33) + 7 = (40) + 8 = (48) +6 = (54)

Now that you know the relationship between the numbers, is it easier to memorize them? Will you be able to keep them in memory for a longer period now?

People can memorize more easily if they find a meaningful relationship or pattern between items.

We also know that most people learn better if they use their imagination to visualize and associate new information in a more meaningful way. Let's use these two techniques on the word list that you have already seen at the beginning of this chapter. How about associating all the words together in an unusual story?

> The crazy island caretaker picked up his toddler son, put sunscreen on his hip, dressed him like an exotic puppet and took him in his canoe to the city where there was a pantomime contest on top of a roller coaster called the Avalanche. Right in the middle of the contest, a stuntman dressed as a slave jumped off the roller coaster and crashed on an anorexic Barbie in high heels on the runway below during a photo shoot.

Imagine this story as a movie and run it a couple of times in your head. Have you now memorized all the words in the correct order?

How about using association and visualization to learn foreign words? The trick here is to think of a word in your first language that sounds similar to the new word and to create a story that links your new word to the word in your language. Let's say you want to memorize the French word *pantalon* (meaning trousers or pants). You can associate the French word *pantalon* with the words *pant* and *alone* in English (*pant + alone = pantalon*). You can now imagine your pants going home alone leaving you without pants on the street. Obviously, the more languages you speak, the easier this becomes. For instance, if you already know that the word *spoon* in Turkish is *kasık*, associating the Serbo-Croatian *kasika* (pronounced *kash-ee-kah*) to the new word becomes almost effortless.

Add attention and repetition to the techniques above and you will see what wonderful memory you possess.

Comprehension

1. Five techniques were mentioned in this article as memory tricks. Write them below. (The first one has been done for you as an example

1. *Finding patterns*	4.
2.	5.
3.	

2. Try to memorize the following numbers using the pattern technique you learned in the reading passage. Remember—you have to find the relationship between the numbers first.
   a) 3, 9, 27, 81, 243, 729
   b) 25, 24, 22, 19, 15, 10
   c) 3, 5, 8, 13, 21, 34

3. Use association and visualization to memorize the 10 words in each set in the correct order (three minutes to study and three minutes to recall for each set).

Set 1	Set 1	Set 2	Set 2
Blind		Busy	
Neurologist		Gerontologist	
Dementia		Avid	
Store		Knitter	
Brain		Ship	
Savant		Recall	
Refrigerator		Childhood	
Pants		Rhyme	
Random		Lion	
Monitor		Depression	

4. Use the tricks for learning foreign vocabulary to learn the names of the regions of the brain. Study the picture for four minutes. Then cover the picture on the left and write the labels on the picture on the right.

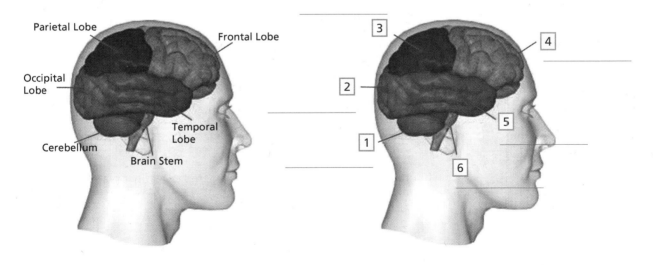

Vocabulary

Personal Data Assistant (PDA)

Knotted string

To acquire	To gain something by your own efforts
Ad infinitum	(from Latin) Without ever coming to an end; endless
Bottom line	The essential point in a discussion
Blurry	Not clear
Clutter	A lot of things in an untidy state, especially things that are not necessary or are not being used; a state of confusion
To delegate	To give a less-important part of your work or responsibility to a person (or a machine) in a lower position
Domain	An area of knowledge or activity; especially one in which somebody is an expert
Fragility	Being delicate and fragile (easily broken)
Method of loci	A trick to memorize the order of or relationships between items by imagining them in familiar locations such as different rooms in our house
Prosthetic	An artificial part of the body; for example a leg, an eye, or a tooth
Scaffolding	Building concepts or ideas on top of one another from easy to difficult
Shifting the problem	To make one problem go away only to be replaced by another problem
Trivia	Facts about many subjects that are used in a game to test people's knowledge

Warm-Up Questions

1. How many telephone numbers do you know by heart?
2. Do you think we memorize more or less information than our ancestors?
3. Do you think technology makes people stupider?

The Outboard Brain

Exercise A

Listen to the audio clip once and circle *T* if the statement is true or *F* if it is false. Also correct the false statements.

1. The expression "outboard brain" refers to techniques and gadgets we use such as cellphones, pocket computers, and online storage to keep track of information instead of memorizing them.   T   F
2. The ancient Incas used knotted strings to play games.   T   F
3. One of the guests on the program (Eszter Hargittai) uses her camera to help her memory.   T   F
4. According to Nora Young, the host of the program, the outboard brain solves our memory problems completely.   T   F
5. According to Saul Greenberg, paper and pencil are less secure and more fragile than the devices we use.   T   F
6. In the old days the limit on information was physical, but we can now store digital information ad infinitum.   T   F
7. Pile-based interfaces force us to name everything carefully and organize them into   T   F
   neat folders.
8. According to Clive Thompson there is a possibility that we lose our mental discipline if we stop memorizing things.   T   F
9. According to Patrick Davidson there is not a lot of value in memorizing trivia.   T   F
10. This program recommends memorizing everything and not using the outboard brain.   T   F

Exercise B

Listen to the program again and complete the following tasks.

1. Fill in the blanks (one word for each blank):

When it comes to keeping track of stuff, sometimes we do that just by remembering things, but often we do that by _a_ _____ them, like you go to the _b_ _____ and you take pictures, or you write down the list of _c_ _____ you need.

Eszter Hargittai uses her camera to take pictures of the _d_ _____ label. If she is in a bookstore she takes a picture of the book's _e_ _____ and _f_ _____ to research it later. She also takes a picture of _g_ _____ _____ where she parks her car. She takes a snapshot of her computer _h_ _____ when she checks maps at home instead of printing the map.

2. Complete these sentences (several words for each blank):
    a) According to Saul Greenberg, computers have changed not only the amount we have to remember but also what we have to remember. For example we now have to remember computer-related facts such as passwords, _____ _____. (name at least three items)
    b) According to Patrick Davidson, the more we learn about a specific domain, the easier it becomes to _____ knowledge.
    c) To memorize better, Davidson recommends scaffolding or piling tricks such as visualization and _____ . (name at least two more tricks)
    d) (Nora Young) Bottom line: if it's important to remember, _____ _____ ;if not, _____ _____ outboard brain.

Speaking

Role Playing: Have you ever . . .

Work in teams of two. Take turns.

Exercise A

One of you becomes a doctor. The other person is a patient with memory problems.

The doctor goes over the following checklist and asks questions starting with "Have you ever . . .?"

If the answer to any of the questions is yes, the doctor follows up with questions such as "How long have you . . .," "When did the symptoms start?," "How often . . .," etc. The doctor takes notes during the assessment. At the end of the assessment, the doctor makes a diagnosis and gives advice.

Symptom	Frequency	Notes
Migraine headache	never/sometimes/frequently	
Dizziness	never/sometimes/frequently	
Fainting	never/sometimes/frequently	
Convulsions or fits	never/sometimes/frequently	
Nervousness	never/sometimes/frequently	
Sleeplessness	never/sometimes/frequently	
Depression	never/sometimes/frequently	
Change in sensation	never/sometimes/frequently	

Symptom	Frequency	Notes
Poor coordination	never/sometimes/frequently	
Weakness or paralysis of muscles	never/sometimes/frequently	
Mood changes	never/sometimes/frequently	
Behaviour changes	never/sometimes/frequently	
Problems speaking	never/sometimes/frequently	
Problems writing	never/sometimes/frequently	
Problems making decisions	never/sometimes/frequently	
Getting lost while walking or driving	never/sometimes/frequently	
Losing track of time	never/sometimes/frequently	

Example:

> Have you ever had migraine headaches?
>
> How long have you been experiencing these headaches?
>
> How often do you get them?
>
> When was the last time you had a headache?

Exercise B

One of you becomes a mechanic. The other person is trying to get a used car certified.

The mechanic goes over the following checklist and asks questions starting with "Have you ever . . . ," or "Did you . . . ."

If the answer to any of the questions is yes, the mechanic follows up with questions such as "How long have you . . . ," "How many times have you . . . ," "When did you . . . ," "How often . . . ," etc. The mechanic takes notes during the assessment. At the end of the assessment, the mechanic explains why he cannot certify the car and tells the owner what needs to be done on the car.

Question	Answer	Notes
Accidents?		
Engine repair?		
Transmission repair?		
Passed last emission test?		

Question	Answer	Notes
Leaks?		
Body repair?		
Hesitation or acceleration problems?		
Grinding noises when braking?		
Odometer changed?		
Vibrations at high speed?		
Wind noise while driving with closed windows?		
Rust proofing?		
Trouble closing any of the doors or the trunk?		
Electrical problems?		
How many previous owners?		

Idiomatic and Fixed Expressions

The expressions and idioms used in the following sentences are related to memory. They are missing some words. Read the examples and fill in the blanks with the words from the box. Then guess each idiom's meaning and finally check your dictionary to see if you guessed right.

lane	eye	back
jog	commit	slipped
blank	elephant	stuck
springs	sight	dead
sieve	rack	

Meaning	Example
	You don't remember my name! Let me _____ your memory. It starts with *M*.
	These numbers are very important. I want you to _____ them to memory.
	My grandmother never forgets anything. She has a memory like an _____ .
	My brother is very forgetful. He has a memory like a _____ .
	I can't stop worrying about next week's test. It's always at the _____ of my mind.
	I studied very hard for the test, but during the exam my mind went _____ .
	Sorry I forgot to call you. It totally _____ my mind.
	That song was so memorable that it _____ in my mind forever.
	What's the first thing that _____ to your mind when I say the word *intricate*?
	I saw my ex-girlfriend on the street the other day. She didn't even recognize me. As they say, "out of _____, out of mind!"
	Close your eyes and picture a beautiful garden in your mind's _____ .
	By the time I get home I'm so brain _____ that the only thing I can do is to watch TV.
	I know that girl, but no matter how hard I _____ my brain, I can't remember her name.
	Yesterday, I saw my old high-school friend after several years. We sat down, took a trip down memory _____ and recalled the good old days.

Canadian Outlook

Mental Diseases, Disorders, and Injuries in Canada

One in three Canadians (approximately 10 million people) will experience a disease, disorder, or injury of the brain, spinal cord, or nervous system (neurological or psychiatric) at some point in their lives.

Three percent of (or nearly 1 million) Canadians live with a severe and persistent mental illness. Four thousand Canadians per year will end their life through suicide.

Mental illness is the second-leading cause of hospital admission among those 20–44 years of age.

The World Health Organization (WHO) estimates that by 2020, depression will be the leading cause of disability in developed countries such as Canada.

In teams of two or three study the following list and discuss what symptoms the disorders and diseases may cause. Check in a dictionary if needed. Then research which institution(s) in Canada will be able to help people with each of the conditions below. The first one has been done as an example.

Condition	Symptoms	Organization/institution
Alzheimer's disease	*Memory loss, confusing time or place, inability to solve problems, language problems, etc.*	*Family doctor, Alzheimer's Society of Canada*
Depression		
Down's syndrome		
Multiple sclerosis (MS)		
Obsessive-compulsive disorders (OCD)		
Panic disorders		
Parkinson's disease		
Schizophrenia		
Stroke		
Substance abuse		

Writing

Reports Based on Notes

Prepare a short report (in one or two paragraphs) based on the notes you took for the speaking exercises on pages 92–94.

Sample sentences:

Mr. Zhao has been experiencing severe headaches and dizziness for over a year.

His family members have been complaining about his mood swings for the past six months.

He has lost his way back home three times in the past two months although he always takes the same route home.

The left rear door has been repaired and painted.

There are rust marks on the edge of the right front fender.

The engine has been repaired twice.

The car has had four previous owners.

Chapter 6

Postcards from Canada

Test Your Knowledge of Canada

Read the statements below and decide if they are true or false. Share your answers with other classmates and correct the false statements in teams of two.

1. Christopher Columbus had landed in North America well before the Vikings came to Canada. T F

2. Toronto had been under kilometres of water for more than a million years until the water started to recede about 10,000 years ago. T F

3. Early European explorers had thought that there was no other continent in the Atlantic Ocean between Europe and Asia. T F

4. The Inuit had been making and using ice houses long before refrigerators were invented. T F

5. By the time British Columbia joined Canada in 1871, all other provinces had already joined the Canadian Confederation. T F

Reading

Warm-Up Questions

1. When did Canada become a nation?
2. What does the word *Canada* mean?

Vocabulary

Exercise A

Fill in the blanks in the following verb chart. Check the dictionary for verbs you don't know.

Meaning	Infinitive	Past	Past Participle
to take control of a country by force	to occupy		
			met
		fled	
	to bring		
			sought

Exercise B

The jumbled words in the following table are all taken from the following passage. Read the definition of each word and try to write the correct form of the word. The first one has been done as an example. If you cannot find the word, ask your teacher for a hint.

Word	Jumble	Definition
refugee	eeguerf	A person who has escaped from his or her original country because of war, persecution, or natural disasters.
	ernieeurqmt	Something that is required
	tnselemtet	A place where people have come to live and make their homes, especially where few or no people lived before
	eroirtyrt	Land that is under the control of a particular country or ruler
	cdneset	A person's family origins
	ulebrm	Wood that is prepared for use in building, etc.
	tenurs	A political situation in which people are angry and likely to protest or fight
	gaonibrial	Relating to the original people, animals, etc. of a place and to a period of time before Europeans arrived
	stehinuasm	A strong feeling of excitement and interest in something and a desire to become involved in it

History of Canada

Canada is a land of many cultures and many peoples. Aboriginal peoples have occupied the territory now called Canada for several thousands of years. Everyone else, either by birth or by descent, has been an immigrant—we have all come from somewhere else. It has been said that Canada is a "nation of immigrants."

There are three main groups of Aboriginal peoples in Canada: the First Nations, the Inuit and the Métis. There are more than 50 different languages spoken by Canada's Aboriginal peoples, most of which are spoken only in Canada. In fact, the name Canada may have come from the word *Kanata*, which means *a settlement* in the language of the Huron-Iroquois First Nations people.

As a country, Canada came into being on July 1, 1867. This event is known as Confederation. Before 1867, the French arrived first, then the British. Each brought their own language, system of government, laws, and culture. In 1763, after a long war between the British and the French, all of Canada came under British rule and was known as British North America.

In the late eighteenth and into the nineteenth century, during and after the time of the American Revolution, many African Americans and United Empire Loyalists fled the United States for Canada, where British ties remained and slavery had been abolished.

During the mid-to-late nineteenth and early twentieth century, waves of immigrants arrived from Europe, attracted by the opportunity of a new and better life in Canada. Some settled in towns and cities; others worked in factories, mines, and lumber camps. Many were farmers who turned the Prairie region into wheat fields. Immigrants from China, Japan, and India settled mainly in the western provinces during this time. Many immigrants helped build Canada's national railways, which joined the east and west coasts and opened up the interior for settlement.

After both world wars, thousands of Europeans came to Canada as immigrants and refugees and helped build Canada's postwar economy. Canada's experience during and after the Second World War raised awareness of the needs of refugees and the desire of families to be together.

Over the last 50 years, people from all over the globe have sought a better life or have sought refuge in Canada, fleeing civil wars, political unrest, and natural disasters.

Canada still needs the skills, talents, and enthusiasm of newcomers to build our country, together with those who have come before them. All of this has been reflected in Canada's immigration and refugee policies. Today, Canada is home to immigrants from more than 240 countries. Most newcomers decide to become citizens of Canada after they are settled and have met the requirements of Canadian citizenship.

Comprehension

1. Why is Canada often called a "nation of immigrants"?

2. Name the three main groups of Aboriginal peoples in Canada.

3. What is Confederation?

4. What happened in 1763?

5. Name the two groups of people who escaped to Canada from the United States during the late eighteenth and early nineteenth century.

6. Why did most of the new immigrants during the mid-to-late nineteenth and early twentieth century come to Canada?

7. What are the three main reasons refugees leave their homelands?

8. What is the general tone of this passage? Why do you think the writer wrote this passage?

Grammar: Past Perfect and Past Perfect Progressive

Past Perfect

Had + past participle of the verb

Examples:

I had gone. I had talked. I had eaten.

Negative form: I had not (hadn't) gone. She hadn't talked. They hadn't eaten.

Question form: Had you gone? Had she talked? Had they eaten?

The past perfect tense is used to express an activity or situation that was completed before another activity or situation in the past. If there are two activities or situations in the past, the past perfect tense is used for the older activity and the simple past is used for the more recent one.

Manitoba joined Canada in 1870. (Older past action)

British Columbia joined Canada in 1871. (Newer past action)

Manitoba had joined Canada a year before British Columbia joined.

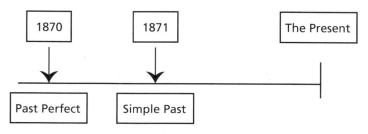

Another example:

The class started at 9:00. (Older past action)

I entered the class at 9:15. (Newer past action)

The class had already started when I entered.

To connect the past perfect and simple past situations, words such as the following are often used:

before	after	when	by the time	because	although

Examples:

I had never seen such cold weather <u>before</u> I came to Canada.

He offered me help <u>after</u> I had solved the problem.

She had already left <u>when</u> the movie finished.

The movie had finished <u>by the time</u> we arrived.

The thief took my computer <u>because</u> I had forgotten to lock the doors.

<u>Although</u> I had studied a lot, I didn't pass the test.

Exercise A

Combine each pair of sentences into one sentence using the words in the parentheses to connect the two parts. Use past perfect for the older action or situation and simple past for the more recent action.

Example:

> The boys ran for about one hour. Then they decided to take a rest. (before)
>
> The boys <u>had run</u> for about one hour before they <u>decided</u> to take a rest.

1. Julie skated all afternoon yesterday. Julie was very tired last night. (because)
2. Mark forgot his dream. Mark woke up. (when)
3. The Vikings left North America. (eleventh century) John Cabot reached North America in the fifteenth century. (before)
4. The Vikings left North America (eleventh century). John Cabot reached North America in the fifteenth century. (after)
5. I told him not to leave. He left. (although)
6. She finished the exercise. She learned to use the past perfect tense correctly. (by the time)

Past Perfect Progressive

Had + been + present participle of the verb

Examples:

> I had been going. I had been talking. I had been eating.
>
> Negative form: I had not (hadn't) been going. She hadn't been talking. They hadn't been eating.
>
> Question form: Had you been going? Had she been talking? Had they been eating?

The past perfect progressive tense is used to express an activity or situation that was in progress before another activity or situation in the past. It emphasizes the duration of the activity.

> Carla had been teaching at the university <u>for 25 years</u> before she retired in 2011.

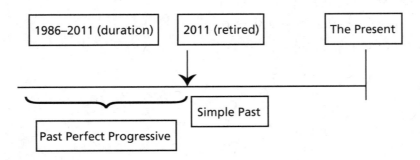

Another example:

> The Inuit had been making and using ice houses long before refrigerators were invented.

Exercise B

Use the simple past, past perfect, or past perfect progressive tenses to complete the following sentences.

Example:

> Kingston _was_ (to be) the capital of Upper Canada before Queen Victoria _chose_ (to choose) Ottawa as the capital of Canada.

The Northwest Passage is a sea route through the islands of northern Canada connecting the Atlantic and Pacific Oceans. For more than three centuries explorers ₁ _____ (to try) to find the route before Norwegian explorer Roald Amundsen finally ₂ _____ (to discover) it in 1906.

At the end of the fifteenth century an Italian named John Cabot who ₃ _____ (to plan) a trip to the New World for several years, ₄ _____ (to sail) to North America after he ₅ _____ (to attract) financial backers in England. Cabot ₆ _____ (to be) as confident as Christopher Columbus ₇ _____ (to be) before him that a new seaway was open to Asia but he never ₈ _____ (to find) it.

In 1531, Francis I of France ₉ _____ (to send) an explorer named Jacques Cartier to look for the route to the Pacific Ocean that Cabot ₁₀ _____ (to fail) to discover in 1497. In 1534, after his second voyage to Canada, Cartier ₁₁ _____ (to send) a complete report to the king of France about the lands he ₁₂ _____ (to see) and the people he ₁₃ _____ (to meet). His reports ₁₄ _____ (to lead) to several other French expeditions.

Grammar Reinforcement

Work in teams of two. Student A makes a grammatically correct question with the words in each set below by adding prepositions, articles, and correct verb tenses. Student B answers. Student A writes down Student B's answers to present to class. Then they switch roles.

Example:

> How many times / try to pass / test / before / finally / succeed?
>
> Student A: How many times had you tried to pass the test before you finally succeeded?
>
> Student B: I had tried it two times before I passed the third time.
>
> Student A (reports): He (or She) had tried the test two other times before he or she finally passed it.

1. Where / study / English / before / come / this school?

2. How long / been / study / English / before / come / this school?

3. Which countries / live / before / come / here?

4. What / hear / this city / before / come / here?

5. What important decisions / make / by the time / finish / high school?

The Film: *Postcards from Canada*

Video Vocabulary

Exercise A

All the nouns below are related to the video you are going to watch. Match the words on the left to their definitions on the right

1. _____ Wilderness	a) Picture, shape, or object that is used to represent a country
2. _____ Glacier	b) Travel a long distance to work
3. _____ Cargo	c) The soft hair that covers the bodies of some animals such as cats
4. _____ Permafrost	
5. _____ Descendant	d) Large natural area of land that has never been developed by man
6. _____ Beaver	e) The plants, flowers, and trees that grow in an area
7. _____ Fur	f) Goods that are carried in a ship or plane
8. _____ Pelt	g) When a type of animal or plant stops existing
9. _____ Emblem	h) A North American animal with thick hair and a flat tail
10. _____ Extinction	i) A large, slow-moving mass of ice
11. _____ Vegetation	j) Ground that is frozen all year round
12. _____ Commute	k) Someone related to another person who lived a long time ago
	l) The skin of a dead animal

Exercise B

Replace each bolded word with one of the adjectives from the list. Check your dictionary if necessary.

sparse	dubious	dull	barren	inhospitable	impassable

1. Some people think that life in the areas near the North Pole is boring.

2. For people used to warmer weather, Canadian winters can be really unwelcoming.

3. The areas near the pole have thin vegetation.

4. Can you believe that there are hot and empty deserts in Canada?

5. The claim that he is a genius is really unreliable.

6. After the 1998 Ontario winter storm, many roads became blocked by fallen trees.

Warm-Up Questions

1. Which country is the largest in the world?
2. Which country is the coldest in the world?

Comprehension

Exercise A

The film you are going to watch is full of statistics about Canada. Watch the film once and fill in the blanks with numbers.

1. Canada has:

    _____ of the world's land.

    _____ of the world's forests.

    _____ of the world's wilderness.

    _____ the world's accessible fresh water.

2. _____ of the Canadian population live on less than _____._____ of the Canadian land mass.

3. More than _____ years ago glaciers covered _____ of Canada, and the spot where Toronto is built today was covered by ice two kilometres thick. The ice finally receded some _____ years ago.

4. Russia out-freezes Canada by an average of almost _____ degree(s) Celsius.

5. The most famous attempt to find the Northwest Passage was made by Sir John Franklin in

    _____ .

6. The average daily temperature in the Canadian Arctic is _____ degrees Celsius.

7. Today Canadian Inuit number around _____ .

8. Nunavut takes up approximately _____ of Canada's land mass.

9. The Inuit have _____ words for snow and ice.

10. Human history in the Arctic spans only _____ years. The Thule people came to the Arctic around _____ years ago.

11. Dinosaurs ruled the earth for about _____ million years until an accident

    _____ million years ago destroyed them. A kind of dinosaur named Tyrannosaurus rex measured _____ metres in height and it weighed _____ tonnes.

12. Number of cars in Canada at the time this film was made: _____

13. Total length of highways in Canada: _____

14. Total kilometres driven by Canadians per year: _____ billion

15. Average time Canadians spend commuting per day: _____ minutes

16. Cost of time lost in traffic per year: _____ billion dollars

17. Average amount of pollutants pumped out per car per year: _____ tonnes

18. Amount of rubber Canadian tire wear puts into the atmosphere each year: _____ tonnes

19. Number of cars Canadians crash per year: _____

20. Number of words Canadians have for this type of transportation: _____

Exercise B

Now watch the film a second time and answer the following questions.

1. According to the narrator at the beginning of the clip, Canada can be divided into two parts. What are these two parts?

2. Look at the population map in the film. Can you identify the two provinces with the largest populations?

3. What is one of the main reasons most of Canada is empty of human population?

4. How did Canada lose its rank as the coldest country in the world?

5. Which country did the early European explorers think they would find by crossing the Atlantic Ocean?

6. Name two cargo items that Sir John Franklin had with him.

7. Name one important item that he hadn't brought with him.

8. What happened to Franklin's expedition?

9. How do Inuit families get most of their food today?

10. When did the Thule culture die out?

11. Which people in Canada are the direct descendants of the Thule?

12. Name two modern tools that the Inuit quickly adopted.

13. Why did Europeans become interested in the Canadian beaver?

14. Why is it hard to find human or animal life in the badlands of Alberta?

15. What are hoodoo rocks?

16. Why are scientists interested in the badlands? What do they look for there?

17. Name four words mentioned on the film as synonyms for the word *car*.

Discussion

Work in teams of two. Discuss the following question:

In the film, it was mentioned that the Inuit have several words for ice and snow. Discuss how a language makes words based on its needs and what the presence or absence of words can tell us about a language or culture. If you speak any other language(s), give examples of words that exist in the other language(s) you know that don't exist in English or vice versa.

Example:

> Like English, many other languages such as Arabic, French, and Spanish have two different third-person pronouns to refer to *he* and *she* while some other languages like Mandarin and Persian have just one third-person pronoun for both genders.

Writing

In one or two paragraphs, introduce the city, town or village in which you were born. You can write about its geographical location, its population, climate, history, main attractions, colleges and universities, major sports teams, or any other interesting information about the place.

Reading

Vocabulary

Exercise A

Match the verbs on the left to their meanings on the right.

1. ___ Determine		a)	To catch people or animals and keep them as prisoners
2. ___ Demonstrate		b)	To take people away illegally and keep them as prisoners, especially in order to get money or something else for returning them
3. ___ Propose		c)	To copy the way somebody speaks, moves, behaves, etc.
4. ___ Engage		d)	To cut words or designs on wood, stone, metal, etc.
5. ___ Escort		e)	To discover the facts about something; to calculate something exactly
6. ___ Capture		f)	To show by your actions that you have a particular quality, feeling, or opinion
7. ___ Manage		g)	To succeed in doing something, especially something difficult
8. ___ Kidnap		h)	To go with somebody to protect or guard them or to show them the way
9. ___ Engrave		i)	To suggest a plan, an idea, etc. for people to think about and decide on
10. ___ Observe		j)	To employ somebody to do a particular job
11. ___ Mimic		k)	To ask for something very firmly
12. ___ Demand		l)	To watch somebody or something carefully, especially to learn more about them

Exercise B

All the vowels are taken out of the following words. Read the definition and complete the spelling of each word.

A person who is the official head of a country or region that is controlled by another country	G _ V _ R N _ R
The act or ceremony of burying a dead body	B _ R _ _ L
The state of suffering and death caused by having no food	S T _ R V _ T _ _ N
An organized journey with a particular purpose, especially to find out about a place that is not well known	_ X P _ D _ T _ _ N
Extremely good; excellent	_ _ T S T _ N D _ N G
A group of 12 of the same thing	D _ Z _ N
A group of people of the same race, and with the same customs, language, religion, etc. living in a particular area and often led by a chief	T R _ B _
A person who catches a person or an animal and keeps them as a prisoner	C _ P T _ R
A dead body, especially of a human	C _ R P S _
A box in which a dead body is buried	C _ F F _ N

Warm-Up Questions

Imagine you are going to another planet where intelligent life exists.

1.   What would you take with you as gifts for the people of that planet?
2.   How would you communicate with them?

The Story of Demasduit (Mary March)

Demasduit

In 1819, Demasduit was captured by John Peyton Jr. who had been paid by the governor of Newfoundland to bring back a Beothuk native. Her husband was killed trying to defend her and his killers measured his corpse to determine the size of someone who could fight half a dozen men. Demasduit was taken to St. John's where she demonstrated an outstanding ability to mimic those around her. She quickly picked up some English and was given the name Mary March. Once she could communicate, she told her captors that she had an infant child. This news caused a wave of protest among local citizens, who wrote to Governor Charles Hamilton, demanding that she be returned to her people and her child. Hamilton hoped that March could become a link between the Beothuk and white settlers in Newfoundland, a way of establishing a diplomatic relationship. Unknown to March or her captors was the death of her baby from starvation, two days after her capture.

The citizens of St. John's proposed to engage 30 men from Twillingate, who were familiar with the woods, to escort her home. Governor Hamilton agreed to the citizens' wishes, but by the time an expedition was mobilized, March had become very ill with tuberculosis. Captain David Buchan headed the expedition, taking March, along with goodwill gifts for her people—36 tin pots, dishes, and kettles; 36 awl blades; 27 looking glasses; 24 knives; and 9 strings of beads—but Buchan could not find her tribe. March said she only wanted to find her child, and then she would return to St. John's. She did not manage either, and died on January 8, 1820.

Wigwam

Buchan thought that returning her body to the site where she had been kidnapped would still represent a gesture of goodwill. He had a coffin built and trimmed with red cloth. Two wooden dolls that Mary March had liked were placed in the coffin and a copper plate engraved with her name was fixed on it. Sixty men went inland with the coffin on a sled, covering eight kilometres a day. After 15 days they found snowshoe tracks that led to a recently abandoned storehouse and wigwams. Five days later they reached the campsite where March had lived. Buchan built a platform and placed the coffin on it with the presents surrounding it. He spent two weeks searching for the Beothuk, without luck. The natives were never far, though. They had been following Buchan, observing his progress. When they were sure that he and his party had left, they took Demasduit's body out of the coffin and placed her in the burial hut that held her husband and child.

Comprehension

1. Why was Demasduit captured?

2. Why did the killers measure the corpse of Demasduit's husband?

3. What special talent did Demasduit show?

4. Why did people ask the governor to return Demasduit to her people?

5. Why did the governor agree to return her?

6. What were Demasduit's people called?

7. Who was Captain Buchan?

8. What did Buchan take with him for Demasduit's people?

9. Why did Demasduit die?

10. Why did Demasduit's child die?

11. What did Buchan do with Demasduit's body?

12. How long did Buchan look for Demasduit's people?

13. Why couldn't Buchan find the natives?

14. What did the natives do with Demasduit's body?

Warm-Up Questions

1. Label the provinces of Alberta and Saskatchewan on the map of Canada below.
2. Can you label any other provinces and territories?
3. What do you know about Alberta and Saskatchewan?

Saskatchewan and Alberta Join Confederation

Exercise A

Listen to the audio and decide whether each of the following statements is about Saskatchewan or Alberta. Circle AB for Alberta and SK for Saskatchewan.

1. This is the eighth province that joined Canada.	AB	SK
2. This is the ninth province that joined Canada.	AB	SK
3. This province has five national parks.	AB	SK
4. This province has more than 100,000 lakes, rivers, and streams.	AB	SK
5. The same political party has held the power in this province for over three decades.	AB	SK
6. W.O. Mitchell was born here.	AB	SK
7. Tommy Douglas was born here.	AB	SK
8. This province is home to Dinosaur Provincial Park.	AB	SK
9. This province does not observe daylight savings time.	AB	SK
10. Gordie Howe was born here.	AB	SK
11. This province has won the Stanley Cup in hockey six times.	AB	SK
12. This province has won the Grey Cup in football three times.	AB	SK
13. This province has won the Grey Cup 19 times.	AB	SK
14. This province is easy to draw.	AB	SK

Exercise B

Listen to the program a second time and answer the following questions.

1. When did Alberta and Saskatchewan join Canadian Confederation? (exact date)

2. Which territory did the two provinces belong to before they joined Confederation?

3. Who were Thomas Walter Scott and Alexander Rutherford?

4. Why do the two speakers argue at the beginning of the program?

5. What is special about Wood Buffalo National Park?

6. What is the name of the book that W. O. Mitchell wrote?

7. What is Gordie Howe famous for?

8. How many times did the Roughriders appear in the Grey Cup?

9. When was Henri Bourassa, the father of Canadian nationalism, born?

10. Why did Terry Fox end his marathon?

11. What happened on September 1, 1985?

12. What was supposed to be called the province of Buffalo?

Speaking

How to Say Numbers

Look at the following numbers and the way they are said in English.

Numerals	Spelled Out
100	one hundred
109	one hundred (and) nine
199	one hundred (and) ninety-nine
1066	one thousand (and) sixty-six
1965	one thousand nine hundred (and) sixty-five
20,984	twenty thousand nine hundred and eighty-four
210,985	two hundred ten thousand nine hundred (and) eighty-five
2,100,970	two million one hundred thousand nine hundred (and) seventy
2,693,234,710	two billion six hundred ninety-three million two hundred thirty-four thousand seven hundred (and) ten

Note: For round numbers between 1100 and 1900, it is very common to read them as eleven hundred, twelve hundred, eighteen hundred, etc. instead of one thousand one hundred, one thousand two hundred, one thousand eight hundred.

Years	Spelled Out
1965	nineteen sixty-five
2002	two thousand and two
1066	ten sixty-six

Fractions	Spelled Out
½	half
¾	three-fourths or three quarters
⅙	one-sixth
2 ³/₇	two and three-sevenths
³⁴⁶/₁₁₉	three hundred forty-six over one hundred nineteen

Decimals	Spelled Out
0.43	zero point four three
3.683	three point six eight three

Exercise A

Take turns reading the following sentences and calculations out loud. If you make a mistake go back and try again until you can read them without any problems.

1. The Gujarat earthquake that occurred on 26 January 2001 at 08:46 AM local time in ndia reached a magnitude of between 7.6 and 7.7 on the Richter scale. Its shock waves spread 700 kilometres. The quake killed around 20,000 people including 18 in Pakistan, injured another 167,000, and destroyed 400,000 homes. More than 600,000 people were left homeless. The worst-hit area was Kutch where 12,220 people died and 80 percent of food and water supplies were destroyed. In the city of Ahmedabad, with a population of 4,600,000, more than 50 high-rises collapsed. Total property damage was estimated at $5,500,000,000 US.

2. The Persian scholar and scientist Al-Biruni (born 5 September 973 in Kath, Khwarezm, died 13 December 1048 in Ghazni) was one of the most learned men of his time. Biruni estimated that the earth's radius was 6,335.725 kilometres (calculated in his book, *The Masudic Canon*)—only 36.211 kilometres less than the modern value of 6,371.936 kilometres.

3. Statistics on the Kingdom of Bhutan
   Total area: 38,394 square kilometres
   Population: 708,427 people (world rank: 165th)
   Population density: 18.4 people per square kilometre
   Population growth: 1.201 percent per year
   Largest city: Thimphu (population: 89,000)
   Life expectancy: 67.3

4. Calculations:
   $\frac{1}{6} + \frac{5}{12} + \frac{3}{4} = \frac{4}{3}$
   $\frac{3}{8} \times \frac{2}{7} = \frac{3}{28}$
   $7.62 - 2.5 + 0.34 = 5.46$

Exercise B

Find statistics for the country of your choice (similar to the ones above for the Kingdom of Bhutan) and present the results orally in class.

Idiomatic and Fixed Expressions

The following expressions and idioms contain numbers and figures. Read the examples and guess each expression's meaning. Check your dictionary if necessary.

Expression	Example
Kill two birds with one stone	I killed two birds with one stone. I needed a car and wanted to sell my old piano. I exchanged my old piano for Jill's car.
Once bitten, twice shy	I'm not going to lend that guy any more money. Once bitten, twice shy!
Double whammy	Terrorist attacks in the middle of the recession! That's a real double whammy!
Two's company, three's a crowd	Jen and Dan asked me to go to the movies with them, but I said no. As the saying goes, sometimes two's company, three's a crowd.

Four-letter word	My children are not allowed to use four-letter words in our house.
Give me five	Wow! Our team won! Give me five! (Slap the palm of my hand with your palm).
(To be) at sixes and sevens	I'm all at sixes and sevens when it comes to math.
(To go) the whole nine yards	My boyfriend went the whole nine yards on Valentine's Day. He took me on a romantic trip to Florida and when we came back, the whole house was filled with fresh roses.
Catch-22	If you don't have Canadian experience, you can't get a job. If you can't get a job here, you will never get Canadian experience. It's a Catch-22.
Ballpark figure	If you're not sure about the exact sales numbers, give me a ballpark figure.

Canadian Outlook

What Defines Canada

If you were asked to name the people, places, events, accomplishments, and symbols that define Canada, who or what would you select?

In teams of two or three, fill in the table below with your top five choices for each category.

Rank	People	Places	Events	Accomplishments	Symbols
1					
2					
3					
4					
5					

Compare your answers to those of other teams in class and discuss the reason for your choices.

On Canada Day 2008, a survey commissioned by Citizenship and Immigration Canada and the Dominion Institute asked a randomly selected sample of 3114 adult Canadians who and what they felt were the 101 people, places, symbols, events, and accomplishments that best define Canada. Check the top five results at the back of the book and compare them to your answers.

Writing

Flashbacks

Use the past perfect or past perfect progressive as many times as possible to develop each of the sentences below into a paragraph by recalling events that had happened before the events in the first sentence.

Example:

> **When we landed in Canada this winter, we were all shocked by the cold weather. On our first visit to Canada as tourists back in July 2008,** we had arrived at the best possible time. We had left all our winter clothing back home and had arranged trips to Niagara Falls and Marineland. It turned out to be one of the best trips of our lives, so our idea of Canada was the one we took home with us that summer. We had heard that Canada could get really cold in the winter, but we had never thought that it would be as cold as this. Well, now we know!

1. When I saw my college professor after so many years, I couldn't recognize her. She had changed so much! Her hair had . . .

2. I felt totally exhausted all day yesterday because the evening before that I had . . .

3. I will never forget the first time I asked her/him out. I had . . .

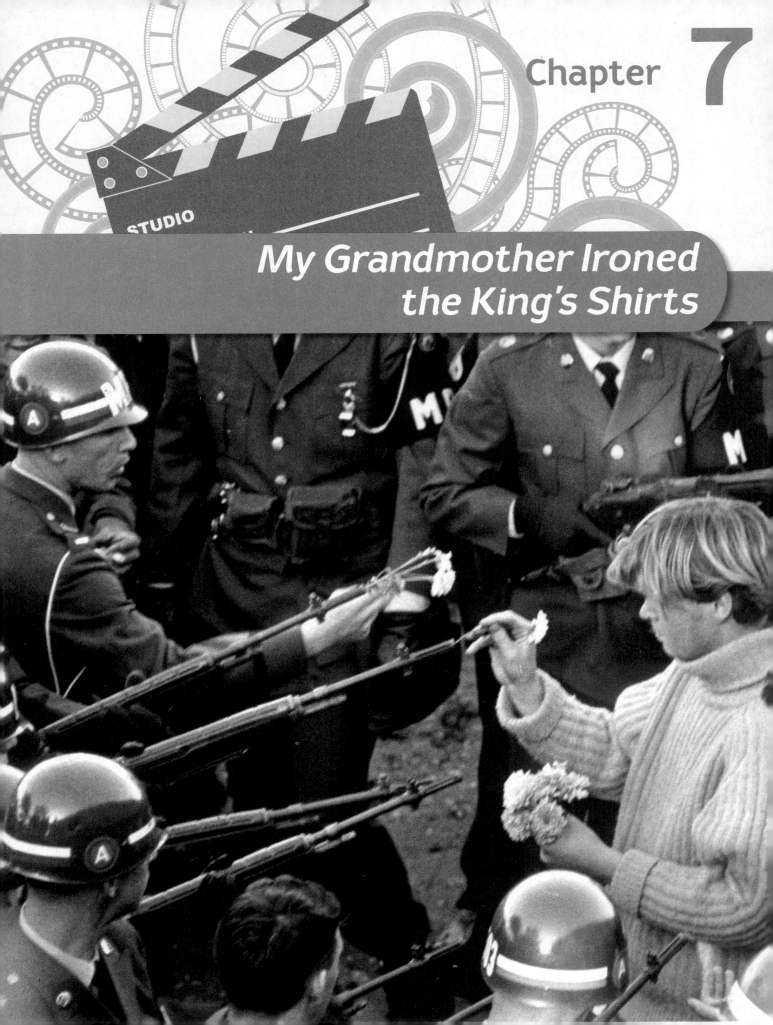

Chapter 7

My Grandmother Ironed the King's Shirts

Introduction

Laws Can Be Crazy

Do you always obey the law? What if the law is so crazy that it is impossible to obey? Will you break or challenge such a law?

Sometimes, lawmakers pass really weird laws and at other times laws that made sense in the past become both useless and irrelevant through time, but lawmakers forget or neglect to remove or change them.

Read the following weird Canadian laws from both the past and the present and in groups of two or three decide why these laws are silly today and why somebody would possibly need to pass such laws.

- For decades, according to the law in certain provinces in Canada, Chinese business owners **could not** hire white females as employees.

- In Ottawa, you **cannot** eat ice cream on Bank Street on a Sunday.

- In Toronto, you **mustn't** drag a dead horse down Yonge Street on a Sunday.

- In Oshawa, Ontario, you **may not** climb trees. It is illegal.

- An Etobicoke, Ontario, bylaw states that you **should not** have more than 3.5 inches of water in a bathtub.

- According to Alberta provincial law, businesses **must** provide rails for tying up horses.

- In Wetaskiwin, Alberta, in 1917, you **had** to tie a male horse a certain distance from a female horse. Tying male and female horses next to each other was considered illegal.

- In British Columbia, you **must not** kill a Sasquatch.

Can you think of other crazy laws you have heard of around the world?

Reading

Warm-Up Questions

Which of the following people do you know of? What do you think they have in common?
- Mahatma Gandhi
- Henry David Thoreau
- Dr. Martin Luther King Jr.

Vocabulary

Read the passage below and find words or expressions that match each of the following definitions.

	To keep complaining about something
	To make something clearer and easier to understand
	To free someone or something from control
	To force liquid or food out of your mouth
	When another country takes control of your country by force
	When a group of workers stop working because they want better pay or working conditions
	Dishonest or illegal behaviour, especially by people in power
	An illegal and often violent change of government
	Cheating in voting
	The act of refusing to listen or to do
	Non-democratic governments that use power unreasonably and don't listen to their people

Civil Resistance

Civil resistance (sometimes called civil disobedience) is non-violent action used by people to challenge a particular power or policy. Unlike violent actions such as war, terrorism, or armed revolutions, the goal of civil resistance is to bring about change through peaceful resistance without hurting others and, if possible, without getting hurt. This can be done in several forms such as slow downs, strikes, and boycotts.

Although it has its roots in ancient history, civil resistance has become more common in modern times and has been used successfully against different forces such as foreign occupations, military coups d'état, dictatorial regimes, electoral fraud, corruption, discrimination, and racism. Mahatma Gandhi used civil resistance to liberate India from British rule and Dr. Martin Luther King Jr. used it to defend the rights of African Americans in what is known today as the civil rights movement.

Sometimes the media use the term *resistance* as a synonym for protest. It is important to note that resistance is more than protest. Resistance is disobedience. Let's clarify this through an example. You ask your nine-year-old son to clean his room. He protests, that is, he argues, nags, or even screams, but when you tell him that he must do it or he will lose his pocket money, he gives up and does what you ask him to do. On the other hand, you want your nine-month-old to eat the food he hates. You push it into his mouth 20 times; he spits it out 20 times. Even when you push it in and hold his nose, he throws up later. He simply refuses to eat it. That's real resistance.

We are all born resistance fighters with a very clear idea of what we like and we don't like, but a lot of us grow up into doubtful protesters at best. The good news is that the resistance fighter is still in us. There is a sleeping Gandhi somewhere in there that can be awakened if called for.

Comprehension

1. What is the definition of civil resistance?

2. What kind of change do civil resistance activists want?

3. What are some examples of violent and non-violent actions? (three examples each)

4. What are two of the situations where civil resistance has been used successfully?

5. Who was the leader of the civil rights movement?

6. How did British rule in India end?

7. What is the main difference between resistance and protest?

8. What do you think the following sentence means? "There is a sleeping Gandhi somewhere in there that can be awakened if called for."

Grammar: Modals of Advice, Necessity, and Prohibition

Advice

Should, ought to, and *had better* are used to give advice or point to the right thing to do. *Should* and *ought to* are synonyms.

> You **should** call the City and complain about your noisy neighbour.
>
> You **shouldn't** give up fighting for your rights.
>
> You **ought to** vote in the next municipal elections.

Had better is stronger than *should* and *ought to*. We often use *had better* to give advice and suggest possible bad consequences if the advice is not followed.

> You'**d better** stay away from violence.
>
> You **had better** let her go or I'll call the police.
>
> We **had better** not talk about this anymore.

Past Advice

To show a suggestion that you didn't follow in the past use *should have, ought to have*, and *could have*.

> You **should have watched** the road more carefully. (Why didn't you?)
>
> I told you not to go out. You **shouldn't have gone**. (Why did you?)
>
> You **could have called** me. (Why didn't you?)

Necessity

Must is used in English to show strong necessity.

> According to Alberta provincial law, businesses **must** provide rails for tying up horses.

We could also use *have to* (both formal and informal) and *have got to* (only informal) to express necessity.

Note: *have to* and *have got to* are not modal verbs.

> I **have to** finish my homework.

> I**'ve got to** finish my homework.

Past Necessity

Must doesn't have a past form. Use *had to* for necessity in the past.

> I **must** work hard today. (present)

> I **had to** work hard yesterday. (past)

> In Wetaskiwin, Alberta, in 1917, you **had to** tie a male horse a certain distance from a female horse. Tying male and female horses next to each other was considered illegal.

Lack of Necessity

Use *don't have to* (*didn't have to* for the past) to show lack of necessity.

> You **don't have to** apologize. It is not your fault.

> You **didn't have to** apologize. It wasn't your fault.

Prohibition

Must not, *may not*, and *cannot* are used to show that something is not allowed. *Must not* (*mustn't*) is very strong and formal.

> In British Columbia, you **must not** kill a Sasquatch.

May not is also formal, but it is not as strong as *must not.*

> You **may not** leave the country until further notice.

Cannot (*can't*) is used in both formal and informal situations to give very strong advice (stronger than *shouldn't*, weaker than *mustn't*).

> You **cannot** smoke in public buildings in Canada.

> In Ottawa, you **cannot** eat ice cream on Bank Street on a Sunday.

Past Prohibition

The past form of *must not*, *may not*, and *cannot* (for prohibition) is *could not* (*couldn't*).

> For decades, according to the law in certain provinces in Canada, Chinese business owners **could not** hire white females as employees.

Summary

Advice	had better (strong), should, ought to
Past advice	should have, ought to have, could have
Necessity	must (strong, formal), have to (weaker, formal and informal)
Past necessity	had to
Lack of necessity	don't have to (present), didn't have to (past)
Prohibition	must not (strong, formal), may not (weaker, formal), cannot (the weakest, formal and informal)
Past prohibition	could not

1. _____ You ought to call your mother from time to time. She really loves it when you call her.	a) Why didn't you?
2. _____ You must report to your manger as soon as you get back.	b) This is something you are expected to do.
3. _____ You don't have to stop at this gas station.	c) You are not allowed to do it.
4. _____ You cannot stop at this gas station.	d) You may do it if you want to.
5. _____ You should have stopped him.	e) Why did you?
6. _____ You didn't have to tell him the truth.	f) This is a strong formal request.

Exercise A

Match each of the sentences on the left with the statement on the right that best describes the sentence.

Exercise B

Fill in the blanks with appropriate verbs from the summary list. You can use positive or negative forms. In some cases more than one answer may be possible.

1. You _____ tell her the truth or I will.

2. You _____ study harder if you want to get good grades.

3. You _____ get 50 percent in order to pass this course.

4. I told you to apply for the scholarship sooner. You _____ applied last month.

5. I thought I would hear from them several days later, but I _____ wait at all. They told me right away.

6. The president _____ leave the country immediately after the coup d'état. They wanted to kill him.

7. What you did to him was wrong. You _____ done it.

8. You _____ be Superman to do this job. Any kid can do it.

9. When we were teenagers, we _____ listen to western music in my country. It was against the law.

10. In most of Canada, you _____ buy alcohol if you are under 19. However, in Manitoba, Quebec, and Alberta you _____ 19 to buy alcohol. You can buy it if you are 18 years old.

Grammar Reinforcement

Travel Advice

Work in teams of two. Your friend wants to travel to a Middle Eastern country and asks for your advice. Use the following information to give your friend some advice. Use modals where possible.

Be alert! There is a constant and high terrorist threat especially around government buildings and tourist attractions.

Avoid religious sites during pilgrimage times. There are safety risks at most religious sites at those times.

Avoid all political gatherings, crowds, and demonstrations.

Keep passports and travel documents in a safe place.

Avoid showing signs of being rich.

Make sure your passport is valid for at least six months after your expected date of departure. Do not carry two passports. Dual nationality is not recognized.

Canadians need a visa to enter the country. You also need a local citizen to sponsor your visa application. There is a heavy penalty for overstaying the duration of your visa.

Avoid wearing shorts or going out without a shirt if you are a man.

Wear a headscarf and full length cloak if you are a woman.

Do not drive a car or ride a bicycle if you are a woman.

Restaurants have two separate sections, one for single men and another for women and families. Go to the appropriate section.

Dancing, music, and movies are prohibited.

Example:

You should be alert at all times especially when you are around government buildings or tourist attractions.

You cannot drive a car or ride a bicycle if you are a woman.

Switch roles. This time your partner gives you travel advice for his or her country of origin.

The Film: *My Grandmother Ironed the King's Shirts*

Video Vocabulary

All the words and expressions below are related to the video you are going to watch. In teams of two, go over the list to see how many of the words and expressions you have heard before. Check your dictionary for those you don't know.

referendum	crisis	surrender	king's subjects
era	cavalier	invader	plea
rightful heir	flee	urge	sabotage
troops	mobilize	devastating	impact
compatriot	resign	approve	impeccable

Warm-Up Questions

1. Can you locate Norway on the map of Europe? How many other countries can you name?

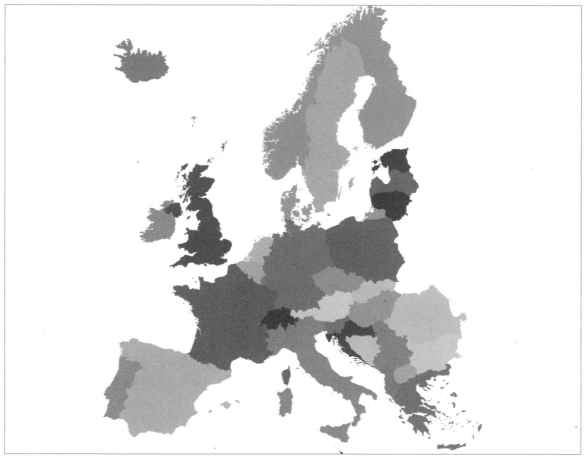

2. Which side of the war was your country of origin on during the Second World War?
3. What is a tall tale? Have you ever told or heard a tall tale?

Comprehension

Exercise A

The animated film you are going to watch is a tall tale (exaggerated story) of an episode in Norway's history as seen through the eyes of the narrator's grandmother.

Watch the complete film once, and in your own words, write a short summary of the story below (maximum of 100 words).

Exercise B

Watch the beginning of the film again and fill in the blanks with the correct information.

1. Norway became an independent country in the year _____ after a national referendum.

2. In the Viking era Norway had lots of kings, most of whom died in bloody _____ over _____ or _____, but there had not been a Norwegian king or queen since King Haakon _____ died centuries ago.

3. Finally, Prince Carl of _____ was selected to be King Haakon _____ of Norway.

4. The new king was very motivated and _____ quickly to the Norwegian way of life, but neither the queen nor the king had ever learned to iron shirts.

5. On May _____ this became a problem when a crowd was waiting for the new king and queen to come out and wave from the balcony.

6. Well, after this _____, they found a respectable clothing shop which agreed to iron their shirts.

Exercise C

Now watch the second part of the film and answer the following questions.

1. How did Grandmother realize that she had been ironing the king's shirts?

2. Why did the king flee from Oslo to Hamar?

3. What is Hamar famous for today? What happened there recently?

4. Why did the king leave Hamar? Where did he go from Hamar?

5. What did he tell his people before leaving?

6. How did Grandmother and her friends at Haff (the clothing shop) show resistance to the enemy?

7. When and why did Grandma resign from Haff?

8. What did the narrator's grandfather say when she asked him how he learned so much about horses?

Hyperbole (Exaggeration)

Writers sometimes use exaggeration to produce comic effect. The story of the film you watched is very funny mainly because certain facts are exaggerated so much that they are almost unbelievable, for example, choosing a king by placing an ad in the royal newspaper.

Watch the complete film again, if necessary, to answer the following questions.

1. Can you find any other hyperbolic moments in the film?
2. Which part of the film was the funniest to you? Why?

Compare answers with your classmates.

Writing

Have your parents or grandparents told you any tall tales about themselves? Have you heard other tall tales that you remember? Write a short piece about the best tall tale you have ever heard.

Reading

Vocabulary

Exercise A

Can you name the objects in the pictures below?

1. _____   2. _____   3. _____

Exercise B

Read the sentences below and replace the bolded expressions with the words *throughout*, *thus*, *eventually*, and *despite*.

Even with killing many innocent people **all over** the country, the British could not push Gandhi

and his followers towards violence. The non-violent movement continued its efforts, and **as a**

result the British Empire **in the end** had to give the people of India their independence.

Exercise C

Use the correct form of the following verbs to fill in the blanks. Remember to use each verb once only.

To broaden	To become wider
To infuriate	To make very angry
To loaf	To spend time not doing anything
To patrol	To go around an area to check that there is no trouble
To retaliate	To do something bad to somebody because he or she did something bad to you
To roam	To walk or travel all over the place
To trigger	To cause or to make something happen suddenly
To venture	To go somewhere even though you know that it might be dangerous

Widespread fraud during presidential elections ₁_____ non-violent street protests all
over the country that soon ₂_____ to demands for basic human rights. The fact that
people ₃_____ outside and spoke against the regime ₄_____ the authorities.

Military units were sent to 5_____ the streets. Fully armed soldiers 6_____ the streets beating men, women, and children savagely. Even beggars 7_____ on street corners were beaten and arrested. Some people 8_____ by capturing videos of the soldiers beating women and children and they posted the videos online along with messages such as "identify these criminals."

Exercise D

Choose the best answer.

1. I must go home before the curfew.
Curfew is:
    a) the time after which, according to the law, people cannot stay outside
    b) the time when the New Year officially begins
    c) the time right before a tropical storm hits an area

2. The inhabitants of New York were shocked and confused after the attacks.
Inhabitants are:
    a) authorities; people who control or manage a place
    b) protesters; people who are not in agreement with the government
    c) residents; people who live in a place

3. He devoted most of his career to providing shelter for stray dogs and cats.
Stray means:
    a) injured
    b) sick
    c) homeless

4. It was past midnight and she was not home yet. He was worried about her. He closed his eyes in a vain attempt to go to sleep.
Vain means:
    a) useless
    b) painful
    c) repeated

5. The manager discussed the new tactics with his team.
Tactics are:
    a) sales numbers and statistics
    b) training material and safety measures
    c) particular methods used to achieve a purpose

6. His biggest achievement as mayor was the development of an urban green zone.
Urban means:
    a) related to the village
    b) related to the city
    c) related to the country

Warm-Up Questions

1. Do you trust the news on TV or in newspapers?
2. How would you react if you found out that most of the political news in your country is nothing but lies?

Strollers Defeat Tanks

On December 13, 1981, the communist authorities in Poland put tanks on the streets to stop the popular resistance movement called Solidarity.

Despite the tanks and arrests, Poles organized protests against the ban on Solidarity, including a boycott of the fiction-filled television news. But a boycott of the TV news could not by itself embarrass the government. After all, who could tell how many were obeying the boycott call?

In one small town, they found a way. Every evening, beginning on February 5, 1982, the inhabitants of Świdnik in eastern Poland went on a walkabout. As the half-hour evening news began, the streets would fill with residents, who chatted, walked, and loafed. Before going out, some placed their switched-off television set in the window, facing uselessly onto the street. Others went a step further. They placed their disconnected set in a stroller or a builder's wheelbarrow, and took the television itself for a nightly outing.

"If resistance is done by underground activists, it's not you or me," one Solidarity supporter later noted. "But if you see your neighbours taking their TV for a walk, it makes you feel part of something. An aim of dictatorship is to make you feel isolated. Świdnik broke the isolation and built confidence."

The TV-goes-for-a-walk tactics, which spread to other towns and cities, infuriated the government. But the authorities felt powerless to retaliate. Going for a walk was not, after all, an official crime under the criminal code.

Eventually, the curfew was brought forward from 10 PM to 7 PM, thus forcing people to stay at home during the 7:30 news, or risk being arrested or shot.

The citizens of Świdnik responded by going for a walk during the earlier edition of the news at 5 PM instead.

Comprehension

1. Why did Poles decide to boycott television news?

2. Which techniques did the people of Świdnik use to show that they were not watching the news? (name three)

3. According to the Solidarity supporter in the reading passage, what is the main goal of dictatorships? How did the people of Świdnik break this goal?

4. What tactic did the government use to stop the boycott?

5. What did the people do in response to the government's new move?

Warm-Up Questions

1. Which animals are considered to be very dirty in your culture?
2. Do people use the names of these animals to insult one another?

Read the passage below and answer the questions that follow.

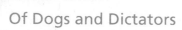

Of Dogs and Dictators

In September 2007, tens of thousands took to the streets to protest against the lawlessness of the military regime in Burma (officially known as Myanmar). The protests were triggered by a sudden sharp increase in the cost of fuel, but quickly broadened to calls for basic rights and freedoms. The military beat, arrested, and killed protesters. According to the UN, at least 31 people died. It became too dangerous to venture onto the streets, which were patrolled by the military. But the imaginative Burmese found a way around that problem: In Rangoon and other cities, they promoted [. . .] stray urban dogs to the ranks of protesters.

Dogs are regarded as lowly creatures in Burmese culture. Being reborn as a dog suggests that you were up to no good in a previous life. [. . .] Stray dogs began to be seen roaming around Rangoon with pictures of the military leader, Than Shwe, and images of other senior leaders tied around their necks, Throughout the city [. . .] troops were seen chasing the [dogs], in a vain attempt to rescue the general's [. . .] low esteem.

Comprehension

1. What started the 2007 protests in Burma?
2. How did the protests change?
3. What did the military do to protesters?
4. Why did protesters use street dogs to show their protest?
5. What did they do with the dogs?

Group Exercise: Help People Fight for Their Rights

In teams of three or four, find as many creative non-violent solutions as you can for each of the following situations. Explain what people **must**, **could**, and **should** do to solve their problems peacefully.

A. Censorship

The government of country A controls and censors all books, magazines, and newspapers that are published in the country. The dictators threaten authors and publishers so that they write and publish only material that is in the government's favour. If unfavourable material is published, authors go to jail and publishers lose their permit to publish or sell books.

B. Environment

The relatively democratic government in country B needs money badly. The parliament has agreed to let a big multinational logging corporation start cutting trees in one of the forests in the country that is home to several rare animals and plants. Police are at the site to control any members of the public trying to stop the work.

C. Minorities

There are two groups of people in country C. One group is the ruling majority, which makes the rules and controls the country. The second group is the minority (racial, religious, etc.). All the laws are in favour of the majority. The members of the majority do not marry, or even do business with, the minority—they are considered unclean. Anybody from the majority dealing with the minority is considered a traitor and is banned from the ruling group.

Listening

Warm-Up Questions

1. What does the word *genocide* mean?
2. What happened to Jews during the Second World War? Why?
3. Can you give more examples of genocide in modern history?

Nonviolence: Twenty-five Lessons from the History of a Dangerous Idea

Exercise A

Listen to the recording once and decide whether the following statements are true (T) or false (F). Also correct the false statements.

1. During the Second World War more Jews were saved by non-violence than by violence.   T   F

2. Germans occupied Denmark because Denmark joined the Allies.   T   F

3. During the strike in the city of Odense in Denmark, four people were killed.   T   F

4. The angry people in Odense killed a German soldier.   T   F

5. Germans announced their decision to deport Jews from Denmark in 1943.   T   F

6. Danes took hidden Jews by boat to Norway.   T   F

7. Because of the Danish government's attention and efforts, no Danish Jews were sent to Auschwitz.   T   F

8. The government of Bulgaria saved its Jewish population by co-operating with Germans.   T   F

9. Raoul Wallenberg was the Swedish ambassador to Bulgaria.   T   F

10. André and Magda Trocmé hid Jewish children and sent them to Switzerland.   T   F

Exercise B

Listen to the recording again and provide the requested numbers and percentages below.

1. Total number of Danish Jews: _____
2. Number of refugee Jews in Denmark: _____
3. Number of Danish Jews deported to Theresienstadt: _____
4. Number of Danish Jews who died (of sickness): _____
5. Total number of French Jews: _____
6. Percentage of French Jews who died: _____
7. Total number of Jews in the Netherlands: _____
8. Fraction of Jews from the Netherlands who died: _____
9. Total number of Polish Jews: _____
10. Percentage of Polish Jews who died: _____
11. Number of Jews saved by Raoul Wallenberg: _____
12. Number of Jewish children saved by André and Magda Trocmé: _____

Exercise C

Fill in the blanks based on what you heard. The first one has been done for you as an example.
During the German occupation, Danes showed different forms of civil resistance such as

1. working . . . _slowly_ _____
2. delaying . . . _____
3. destroying . . . _____
4. protecting . . . _____
5. demonstrating against . . . _____
6. sabotaging . . . _____

Exercise D

Which of the statements below best describes the main message of the recording?

a) During the Second World War, more Jews were saved by non-violence than by violence.
b) Dictatorships are prepared to crush armed resistance. It is non–co-operation that confuses them.
c) If it wasn't for people like Wallenberg and the Trocmés, many more Jews would have died during the war.
d) Many Jews lost their lives during the war simply because they tried to use violence against a stronger enemy.

Idiomatic and Fixed Expressions

The following expressions are related to the subject of resistance. Which ones have you heard before? What do you think they mean?

Expression	Definition
Passive resistance	
(Take) The line / path of least resistance	
Stand / Hold one's ground	
Take a stand against	
Pocket of resistance	
Dig one's heels in	
Stick to one's guns	

Now check your dictionary to see if you guessed right.

Speaking

Advice, Necessity, and Prohibition without Modal Auxiliaries

It is possible to use several other structures besides modal auxiliaries for advice, necessity, or prohibition.

The structures on the left are alternatives for the ones on the right.

If I were you, I would close the door.	I think you'd better close the door.
If I were you, I wouldn't do that.	I think you'd better not do that.
How about working harder?	I think you should work harder.
Try speaking louder.	I think you should speak louder.
Why don't you do it again?	I think you ought to do it again.
Let's try harder.	I think we should try harder.
You are supposed to meet him at eight.	You should meet him at eight.
You are not supposed to be here.	You shouldn't be here.
You weren't supposed to call her.	You shouldn't have called her.
Whatever you do, don't break the speed limit.	You must not break the speed limit.
Don't do it.	You mustn't do it.
You are not allowed to park here.	You cannot park here.
We were not permitted to leave the building.	We couldn't leave the building.
It is forbidden to feed the birds.	You must not feed the birds.
It's necessary to fasten your seat belt.	You must fasten your seat belt.
It was necessary to end the war.	We had to end the war.
You need to bring two pieces of identification.	You must bring two pieces of identification.
It isn't necessary to attend the seminar.	We don't have to attend the seminar.
It wasn't necessary to reapply.	We didn't have to reapply.
You don't need to carry a licence.	You don't have to carry a licence.

Exercise

With a partner, take turns posing and responding to the questions or situations below without using modal auxiliaries.

- I am in love with someone, but don't know how to show my love. What should I do? What shouldn't I do?

- I'm applying for a student/immigration visa. What are some of the conditions I have to meet? What documents do I have to present? What documents or conditions are not necessary?

- I am flying to the United States next week. What are some of the items I cannot take with me on the plane? Is there anything I cannot do before, during, or after the trip?

Canadian Charter of Rights and Freedoms

The Canadian Charter of Rights and Freedoms is a part of the Constitution of Canada that guarantees certain rights and freedoms for all Canadians.

The rights and freedoms are defined under the seven categories in the table below.

As a group, decide what rights and freedoms you think should be included in each category in the table below. When you are done, check your guesses against the Canadian Charter of Rights and Freedoms in the appendix of this book.

Fundamental freedoms	Example: *freedom of religion*
Democratic rights	
Mobility rights	
Legal rights	
Equality rights	
Language rights	
Minority language education rights	

Discussion

1. Do you think there are freedoms and rights that should be added to the Canadian Charter? Why?
2. Do you think there are freedoms and rights that should be deleted from the Canadian Charter? Why?

Writing

Developing an Essay Using a Diagram

You always get good marks because of your excellent planning skills. One of your classmates asks for your advice on what planning strategies to use to become more successful and improve his or her marks.

Use the diagram below to develop an essay. Develop each of the four strategies on the diagram into a separate paragraph and add details to support the ideas by explaining *why* and *how* to do each strategy. Add an introduction and a conclusion to your essay.

Note: Try to use the advice, obligation, and prohibition structures you learned in this lesson.

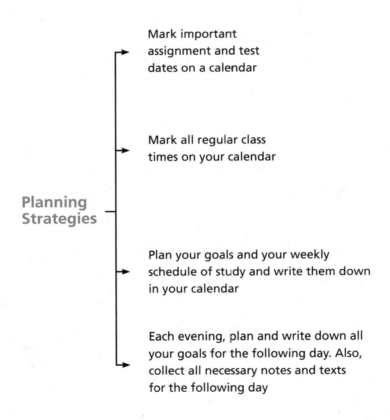

Planning Strategies

- Mark important assignment and test dates on a calendar
- Mark all regular class times on your calendar
- Plan your goals and your weekly schedule of study and write them down in your calendar
- Each evening, plan and write down all your goals for the following day. Also, collect all necessary notes and texts for the following day

Chapter 8

Murder Remembered

Introduction

Solve the Puzzle

Read the following puzzles and in groups of two or three try to solve them. Share your solutions with other classmates.

1. A man, looking at a painting, says to himself: "Brothers and sisters have I none, but that man's father is my father's son." Who **could be** the subject of the painting?

2. Jack lives on the thirtieth floor of an apartment building with his parents. He goes to school by himself, so every morning he takes the elevator all the way down to the ground floor and heads out. When he returns, he takes the elevator up to the twentieth floor and then walks the rest of the way to the thirtieth floor. On rainy days or when there is someone else in the elevator, he takes the elevator all the way to the top. What **may be** the reason for his actions?

3. A young man's body was discovered in a park in Toronto in the middle of summer. He had a fractured skull and many other broken bones, but the main cause of his death was hypothermia. What **could have happened** to the young man?

4. A man wants to reach the island in the middle of the pool (as in the picture below) without getting wet. The island is 20 feet from each edge of the pool. He has two planks, each 19 feet long. How **might** the man use the planks to reach the island?

Do you know any other puzzles you could share with your classmates?

Reading

Warm-Up Questions

1. Have you ever watched TV series such as *CSI* or *Criminal Minds*? What does *CSI* stand for?
2. What does the expression "forensic science" mean?
3. How does science help police solve crimes?

Vocabulary

All the words in the puzzle on the next page are taken from the reading passage below. You can scan the passage for the words.

Anna Maria Schonleben was once married to an abusive, alcoholic lawyer much older than herself, but he died after going through her money, leaving her in *poverty* and *debt*. Already 49 years old and described as a woman without any attraction of face, Anna realized she might have to spend the rest of her life alone and without any financial support. She, therefore, started working as a servant for older gentlemen, hoping she may make them marry her for her cooking and other domestic skills.

She was even ready to kill to get what she wanted, and her *weapon* of choice was a poison called arsenic: If the man she wanted was already married, she could poison his wife.

She started working for a Judge Glaser in Bavaria and soon killed his wife, but he did not marry her. She left the household to find her next *target*, a *widower* named Judge Grohmann. But, Grohmann soon announced his engagement to another woman and Anna who must have felt betrayed, *retaliated* by killing him with a bowl of poisonous soup. She also poisoned two of his servants who fortunately didn't die. Her next victims were the wife and the infant baby of her third employer, a *magistrate* named Gebhard. She also poisoned two of the servants who *suspected* they might have been poisoned and told the judge, so he sent their food and some dishes for analysis. By the time the results for arsenic came back positive, and authorities were alerted, Anna had already escaped.

When Anna was finally arrested on October 18, 1809, the police found some toxic substance in her pockets which was later proved to be arsenic. She was already linked with many *suspicious* deaths and all the investigators had to do was to prove it scientifically. The science of arsenic analysis was very young at that time. In 1806, just a few years before Anna's arrest, a scientist named Valentine Rose had invented a method to prove the existence of arsenic in human body.

Using this new method, chemists found arsenic in the body of Judge Glaser's wife and as they had already discovered arsenic in saltshakers in another household where Anna had worked, the detectives reached the conclusion that Anna must have committed the murders. She confessed to the *homicides* after six months of questioning. She called arsenic "her truest friend" and said she was happy she was arrested as she did not think she could stop killing. She was *convicted* of murder and was *beheaded* in 1811.

Across

3 If you do not trust someone and think that the person has done something wrong, but you do not have any proof, you are _____ of that person.

4 A man whose wife has died and who has not married again is a _____.

6 To decide officially in court that somebody is guilty of a crime

7 Money you owe others

8 State of being poor; not having money

10 To warn somebody about a dangerous situation

11 An object such as a knife, gun, bomb, etc. that is used for fighting or attacking somebody

13 To do something wrong or illegal: He is going to _____ arson.

14 An official who acts as a judge in the lowest courts of law

Down

1 The crime of killing somebody on purpose

2 To cut off somebody's head, especially as a punishment

3 To have an idea that somebody is guilty of something, without having definite proof

5 To do something harmful to somebody because they have harmed you first

9 A person, object, or place selected as the aim of an attack

12 Poisonous

Comprehension

Read the passage on page 137 one more time to find the answers to the following questions.

1. What is a good title for this reading passage? Write the title on the line provided on top of the reading.

2. In what time period did the events of this story happen?

3. Why was Anna worried about her future? (Give at least two reasons)

4. Why did she choose to become a servant?

5. Who did Anna kill in the households of each of the following employers?
   - Judge Glaser
   - Judge Grohmann
   - Magistrate Gebhard

6. Why did Magistrate Gebhard suspect Anna?

7. What did he do after he became suspicious?

8. What happened in each of the following years?
   - 1806
   - 1809
   - 1811

9. How did investigators link the arsenic murders to Anna after she was arrested? (three steps)

10. What did Anna say after she admitted to the murders? Why do you think she thought that way?

Grammar: Modals of Certainty, Possibility, and Impossibility

Certainty: *Will, Must*

Will can be used to make a prediction or an assumption with a high degree of certainty (usually about the immediate or distant future).

> The restaurant is so busy tonight. We **will** need more waiters.
>
> (Prediction based on the number of people coming in)
>
> I just received another text message. It**'ll** be from my crazy boyfriend again.
>
> (Assumption based on the previous messages)
>
> It's no use calling Jack at this time of night. He **won't** pick up. He usually goes to bed at nine.
>
> (Prediction based on Jack's habits)

Must can express strong <u>certainty</u> in the present or the future.

> You were there with me when I talked to her a couple of days ago. You **must** remember.

> You went to bed so late last night. You **must** be sleepy now.

Past Certainty: *Must have*

Must have expresses strong <u>certainty</u> in the past.

> It's wet everywhere. It **must have rained** last night.

> We found traces of arsenic in the victim's stomach. He **must have been** poisoned.

Impossibility: *Can't, Couldn't*

Can't and **couldn't** express <u>impossibility</u> in the present or the future.

> This **can't** be the murder weapon. She was killed by a much heavier object.

> My life is perfect. It **couldn't** get better than this.

Past Impossibility: *Can't have, Couldn't have*

Can't have and *couldn't have* express <u>impossibility</u> in the past.

> Wow! You learned to write in Arabic. It **can't have been** easy to learn such a different system.

> (I'm sure learning to write in such a different language wasn't easy for you.)

> He **couldn't have killed her**. He was in the classroom at the time of the murder.

> (It was impossible for him to kill her since he was in the classroom at that time.)

Possibility: *May, Might, Could*

May, *might,* and *could* are used to suggest possibility. *Could* and *might* are sometimes weaker than *may*.

> He **may/might/could** be the killer, but we don't have any proof.

> There are several explanations for this mystery. Yours **could** be one of them.

> You **could** ask your brother for money. He **might** give you some.

Past Possibility: *May have, Might have, Could have*

Sometimes *might have* and *could have* are weaker than *may have*.

> I can't find my keys. I **may have left** them at home.

> He **could have killed** his partner. He was in the same building at the time of the murder.

> We suspected that she **might have been** poisoned.

Summary

certainty	*will, must*
past certainty	*must have* + past participle
impossibility	*can't, couldn't*
past impossibility	*can't have* + past participle, *couldn't have* + past participle
possibility	*may, might, could*
past possibility	*may have* + past participle, *might have* + past participle, *could have* + past participle

Exercise A

Match each of the sentences on the left with the statement on the right that best describes the meaning of the sentence.

1. _____ This poison must have killed him.	a)	The poison certainly didn't kill him.
2. _____ This poison could have killed him.	b)	This poison almost certainly killed him.
3. _____ This poison could kill him.	c)	Maybe this poison killed him.
4. _____ This poison can't have killed him.	d)	This poison won't kill him.
5. _____ This poison can't kill him.	e)	Maybe this poison will kill him.

Exercise B

Fill in the blanks with appropriate modal verbs from the summary table. Add the correct form of the verbs in parentheses after the modals. In some cases more than one answer may be possble.

Some events are so strange that one ₁ _____ (not, believe) them. The account of Grigori Rasputin's murder is more like a legend. Nobody knows for sure and some parts of the story ₂ _____ (be) exaggerated through time, but I believe some of it ₃ _____ (be) true. Rasputin ₄ _____ (be) a very strong man because his enemies put a large amount of cyanide in his wine, but he didn't die of poison. That much cyanide ₅ _____ (kill) five ordinary men. They then shot him in the back. Again he survived. They shot him three more times. Some of the men were very scared. They said, "He is a monster. He ₆ _____ (not, be) killed." There was no turning back, though. They hoped that he would die of bleeding by morning, but some of them were worried that if they left him like that he ₇ _____ (survive). They wrapped his body in a carpet and threw him into the icy waters of the Neva River.

Three days later his body was found in the river. Based on the results of the autopsy, he ₈ _____ (not, die) of the bullets, because they found water in his lungs—suggesting that he had drowned.

Grammar Reinforcement

Guess What Happened

Work in teams of two. You will be given two problems and some possible solutions for each problem. Using modals discuss the possible causes of each problem. In the end, choose one solution as your favourite and write a summary of your discussion to report to class.

1. Why did dinosaurs become extinct? What happened more than 65 million years ago to kill a species that had survived for 150 million years?

Possible Causes:

asteroid impact
climate change
volcanic eruptions
mysterious disease

2. The Bermuda Triangle is a part of the North Atlantic Ocean where about 50 aircraft and ships disappeared mysteriously. What happened to the ships and planes? Why did they disappear?

Possible Causes:

UFOs and alien abductions
time warp or portal to another dimension
pirates
Gulf Stream currents or hurricanes
exaggerated or false reports

Example:

A huge asteroid **might have hit** the earth. The impact of such a big asteroid **can create** a dust cloud that destroys plant life and blocks the sun for several months. The dinosaurs **couldn't have survived** without sunlight and plant life.

The Film: *Murder Remembered*

Video Vocabulary

All the words and expressions below are related to the video you are going to watch. Match the words on the left to their definitions on the right.

1. ____ Disguise	a) A small building, usually made of wood or metal, that has not been built well
2. ____ Vault	b) A legal document that gives the police authority to do something
3. ____ Ledger	c) An act of stealing (often from a bank) using a gun
4. ____ Bundle	d) A gun with a long barrel that you hold to your shoulder to fire
5. ____ Rifle	e) The act of following or chasing somebody
6. ____ Ditch	f) The act of killing somebody, especially as a legal punishment
7. ____ Interval	g) A book in which a bank records the money it has paid and received
8. ____ Stick-up	h) Fake; made to look exactly like the original
9. ____ Shack	i) A number of things (such as bills) tied or wrapped together
10. ____ Fugitive	j) A thing that you wear or use to change your appearance so that people do not recognize you
11. ____ Counterfeit	k) A person who has escaped or is running away from somewhere and is trying to avoid being caught
12. ____ Execution	l) A room with thick walls and a strong door, especially in a bank, used for keeping valuable things safe
13. ____ Pursuit	m) A period of time between two events
14. ____ Warrant	n) A long channel dug at the side of a field or road, to hold or take away water

Warm-Up Questions

1. What motivates one person to kill another?
2. What would you do if you saw a killer trying to escape?

Comprehension: Clip 1

The film you are going to watch is about a murder-robbery in Canada in 1950. In the first clip, witnesses describe the robbery that happened several decades ago.

Watch the clip once and complete the table of events below as you are watching. Use the cue words in each box to take notes about the events in that particular scene. Write in as much detail as you can. The first one has been done as an example.

2:45 PM	*The robber was waiting in his car at 2:45 on Wednesday afternoon June 21, 1950. He waited until the last customer had left before he entered the bank.*
Cheque in hand / no disguise	
Stick-up / alarm	
Pulled second gun	
Threw bundles of money	
Robber left the bank	
Pursuit	
Shooting / murder	
Escape	

Watch the complete clip a second time; then read the statements below. Circle *T* if the statement is true or *F* if it is false. Also correct the false statements.

1. The bank robber was wearing a sun helmet, sunglasses, a black coat, and a clean work shirt.   T   F

2. He asked everyone in the bank to get into a corner.   T   F

3. The neighbours tried to call the police, but the lines were busy.   T   F

4. He stole about $40,000 from the bank.   T   F

5. Three of the clients in the bank tried to follow the robber until the police arrived.   T   F

6. The people in pursuit shot at the robber's car first.   T   F

7. The robber lost control of his vehicle and hit the other car.   T   F

8. The robber shot at his pursuers with a handgun first and killed them later with a machine gun.   T   F

9. After killing the two men who were following him, the robber escaped on foot through the woods.   T   F

10. The witness to the shooting (Bob) was 14 years old at that time.   T   F

Comprehension: Clip 2

Watch the second clip once or twice and answer the questions. In this part, the criminal is arrested and the police finds out his real name and search his house and garage.

1. Where did Bert, the farmer, find the killer?

2. How many days after the murder was the killer arrested?

3. What were the names of the two people who were killed? (Hint: read the tombstones.)

4. According to the victim's son, why did his dad decide to pursue the robber?

5. How old was his dad when he was killed?

6. How many children did the victim have?

7. Who revealed the real name of the killer to the police?

8. Where did the killer live?

9. What did the police find at the killer's garage?

10. Why did McAuliffe rob the bank?

Comprehension: Clip 3

Watch the second clip once or twice and answer the questions. In this part, the criminal is sentenced to death.

1. How long did the jury take to reach a decision? (Hint: read the newspaper.)

2. How was he going to be killed?

3. What was the exact date set for McAuliffe's execution?

4. Who did McAuliffe write to before his execution?

5. How long before his execution did he write the letter?

6. How much money did he have at the time of his death? What did he do with the money?

7. What word does the police officer use to describe the look on McAuliffe's face at the time of his execution?

8. What did McAuliffe ask the priest to do at the time of his execution?

Discussion

Work in teams of two. Discuss the following questions. Watch the film again if necessary.

1. (Clip 1) Based on the witnesses' descriptions, how was the robber's behaviour? Was he in control of the situation or was he scared? Was he serious about hurting people or was he just pretending?
2. (Clip 2) What do the victim's son and the other local resident (Clarence Abbott) think about the victim's decision to pursue the robber? Do they think it was a wise decision or not? How do you know?
3. (Clip 3) After listening to McAuliffe's last letter before his death, what kind of a person do you think he was? Why do you think so?
4. What is your opinion of capital punishment (killing a criminal for a serious crime)? Do you support or oppose capital punishment? Why?

Writing

Do you know of any high-profile crimes in your culture or country of origin that made headlines? Research the crime if necessary and write a short report (around 150 words) about what happened.

Reading

Vocabulary

Study the words and definitions below before you read the passage that follows.

Casualty	A person who is killed or injured in war or in an accident
Indemnity	A sum of money that is given as payment for damage or loss
Beneficiary	A person who receives money or property when somebody dies
Terminal	Leading to death; ending
Fund	An amount of money that has been saved or has been made available for a particular purpose
Estate	All the money and property that a person owns, especially everything that is left when he or she dies
Probate	Confirmed; proved
Coroner	An official whose job is to discover the cause of any sudden, violent, or suspicious death
Terminate	End; to make something end
Overturn	Turn upside down
Presume	Suppose that something is true, although you do not have actual proof
Defraud	Get money from a person or an organization by tricking them
Felony	The act of committing a serious crime such as murder or rape; a crime of this type

Warm-Up Questions

1. Have you ever heard of *insurance fraud* or *insurance scams*? What do these terms mean?
2. What is a joint insurance policy?

The Case of the Buckle File

There is a mystery hidden in the following letters. First read each letter and answer the comprehension questions that follow it, then go to the section "Solve the Mystery" on page 150 and try to answer the question with the help of your classmates.

BEAVER LIFE AND CASUALTY INSURANCE COMPANY

1 October 2010

Mr. Ernie Buckle
104 West Port William Road
Thunder Bay, ON
P8L V1X

Dear Mr. Buckle:

Re: Joint Life Policy BV 297562
Ernie and Audrey Buckle

I have received your letter of 25 September 2010 and the enclosed forms authorizing the addition to your policy of a double indemnity clause for accidental death.

Please note that Mrs. Buckle has not signed Form 22A. Since yours is a joint policy with you and your wife as each other's beneficiary, it is necessary that both of you sign. Accordingly, I am returning Form 22A for her signature.

Further, you have not designated a beneficiary to receive the indemnity should it occur that you and Mrs. Buckle encounter a terminal accidental event together. The funds, if such were to occur, would thus be paid to your respective estates on a 50/50 basis, and would therefore be subject to probate fees and taxation. If this is your wish, you and Mrs. Buckle must initial clause 12 on page 2 of Form 22A. However, should you wish to designate a beneficiary, please enter his/her/their name(s) and address(es) in the space below clause 13 on page 2.

I will hold your cheque until I receive the completed Form 22A, and other instructions on the above matters.

Sincerely,

Christine Cooper
Client Services

Comprehension

Exercise A

1. Why did Christine Cooper send this letter?

2. What two changes did she ask the Buckles to make on Form 22A?

Oct. 12/10

Beaver Insurance Co

Dear Miss Cooper,
Here is the form with my signature that you asked for. Sorry I didn't do this before. Ernie usually is the one who looks after these things. Also like you said, for ~~beneficiaries~~ beneficiary we picked my cousin Reenee Clubek in Lybia.

Hope this is alright now.

Audie Buckle

3. Why hadn't Audrey (Audie) signed the forms before?

4. What can you tell about the writer of this letter by looking at her grammar, spelling, and language in general?

BEAVER LIFE AND CASUALTY INSURANCE COMPANY

12 November 2010

Mr. Ernie Buckle
Mrs. Audrey Buckle
104 West Fort William Road
Thunder Bay, ON
P8L V1X

Dear Mr. and Mrs. Buckle:

Re: Joint Life Policy BV 297562

Enclosed please find notice of confirmation regarding changes to the above policy, with copies for your files. The changes are effective as of 15 October 2010.

Sincerely,

Signature: Jack Hall for Christine Cooper
Christine Cooper

5. Why did Christine Cooper send this letter?

July 29, 2011

Ms. Christine Cooper
Beaver Life and Casualty

<u>BY FAX</u>

Your telephone message of 27/07/11 handed to me this AM. Body of Ernie Buckle recovered from Wabakimi Lake at 3:15 PM, 25/07/11. Coroner has ruled accidental death by drowning. No inquest scheduled.

Search for body of Audrey Buckle terminated this AM. Overturned canoe located in Wabakimi established as belonging to the Buckles. No further search planned. Status of Audrey Buckle is "presumed dead."

We will have full reports available by 10/08/11. You can get these through usual channels from district headquarters in Thunder Bay.

Constable Allan Longboat
Ontario Provincial Police
Search and Rescue Unit
Sioux Lookout

6. What is the responsibility of this letter's sender?

7. Why did he send this letter?

8. According to this letter, why did the Buckles die?

9. Why is Audrey Buckle presumed dead? Why presumed?

March 18, '12

To Whom It May Concern,
Beaver Life and Casualty Insurance
7272 Barton Street
Hamilton, Ontario
CANADA

VIA AIR MAIL

Dear Sir or Madam,

I am writing in regard to the deaths of Ernie and Audrey Buckle. As you know, I am the beneficiary named in the life insurance policy they held with your company.

Very shortly I will be moving from Lybia to a project in East Africa. My new address, effective March 31, '12 will be

c/o Central Postal Station
Box 241
Haile Selassie Blvd.
Nairobi 17
KENYA

It would be helpful if you could tell me when the policy benefit will be issued.
I appreciate your help in this matter.

Sincerely,

Irene Clubek

10. Who wrote this letter?

11. Why did she write the letter? (two reasons)

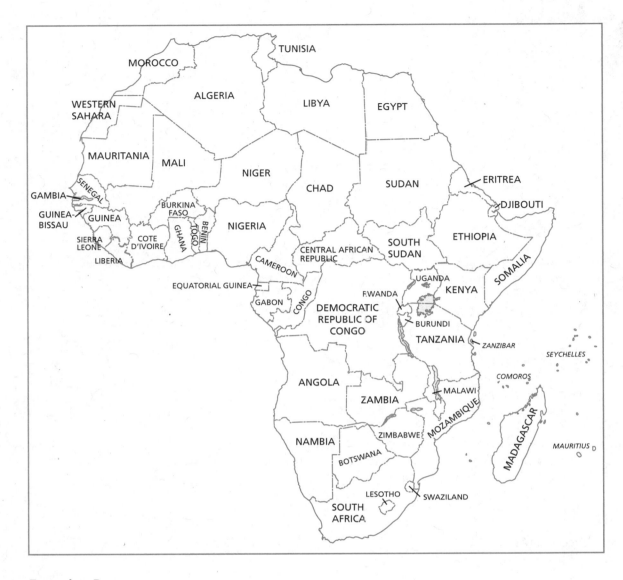

Exercise B

Solve the Mystery

On April 2, 2012, Christine Cooper wrote a memo to her immediate superior stating that one item in particular made her feel that Beaver Life and Casualty was being defrauded in this case, and that the case might also involve a felony. What made her feel that?

Listening

Vocabulary

The following words are related to crime and law. Study their definitions before listening to the report.

Court / courtroom	A place where crimes are judged
Prisoner's box	The place in a court where the prisoner stands or sits
Trial	A formal court session to see if a person is guilty or not
Hearing	A formal meeting where the facts about the crime are presented to decide if the file should be sent for trial or not
Accused	The person or persons on trial for committing a crime
Victim	Someone who has been attacked, hurt, or killed in a crime
Witness	A person who sees the crime happen
Prosecutor	A lawyer who leads the case against the accused
Justice	The title used before the name of a judge; for example, Justice Jeffries
Lay a charge	Make an official claim that somebody has committed a crime
Plea	A statement made by the accused accepting or not accepting guilt
Plead guilty / innocent	Make a statement and accept or reject guilt
Sentence	Announce officially the punishment for a crime
Serve a sentence / serve time	Receive the punishment; to go to prison for a crime
Parole	Permission that is given to a prisoner to leave prison before the end of their sentence on condition that they behave well
The crown	The government of the country representing the queen
Premeditated murder	Murder that is planned in advance

Warm-Up Questions

1. Have you ever heard the expressions *crime of passion* and *honour killing*? What do they each mean?
2. Have you ever witnessed a crime in progress? If yes, how did you react? Did you try to help directly or did you call for help? Which one is better?

The Second-Degree Murder Trial of Jason Getson

Exercise A

You are going to listen to the first part of a report about the murder of a young woman in eastern Canada. After listening to the clip, provide the requested information about the people involved.

The Accused

Name: *Jason Getson*

Age:

City:

Time of arrest:

Place of arrest:

First charge:

Final charge:

Plea:

The Victim

Name:

Age:

Relationship to the accused:

Number of wounds:

Cause of death:

Exact location of the crime:

Exact date and time of the crime:

Parents' names:

Number of brothers and sisters:

The Witnesses

Number of people who called 911:

Where was the victim when the first witness noticed her?

What did the witness think at first?

How did she call the police?

Where was the second witness when she heard screams?

Where was the victim when the second witness saw her?

How did she call the police?

Exercise B

Listen to the second part of the report and match each event with the date when the event happened. The first one has been done as an example.

Date	Event
1. _a_ December 2010	a) Jason went to court for the hearing.
2. _____ 1997	b) Jason killed Melanie.
3. _____ October 2004	c) Jason will receive his sentence.
4. _____ December 2009	d) Melanie started dating Jason.
5. _____ March 2010	e) Melanie told Jason that she was leaving him (for a second time).
6. _____ Late April 2010	f) Melanie left Jason for the first time and called a lawyer for divorce
7. _____ May 8, 2010	g) Melanie and Jason got married.
8. _____ May 10, 2010	h) Jason bought two knives and three sets of handcuffs from the Canadian Tire
9. _____ January 4, 2011	i) The couple reconciled (got back together).

Exercise C

Listen to the second part of the report again and answer the following questions.

1. What was one of the main reasons Melanie separated from Jason?

2. Where did Jason work? What was his job title?

3. What are the definitions of first- and second-degree murder charges?

4. What is the sentencing difference between first- and second-degree murders in Canada?

5. How did Jason act during the trial?

6. How did he act right after the murder?

Discussion

1. Jason and Melanie had been together for a long time. What do you think caused Jason to kill Melanie?
2. How could he kill his love of so many years?
3. After the murder, Jason told his brother that he was going to kill himself. Why did he want to kill himself and why do you think he didn't do it?
4. How do you explain the difference between Jason's reaction at the time of the killing and his reaction in the courtroom?

Speaking

Probable or *Possible*

Possible is weaker than *probable*. In other words, when something is probable, there are more chances it will happen than when it is possible.

Exercise A

The table below contains expressions that show different degrees of certainty. The ones on top are more probable than the next ones. Write an example sentence for each expression. For example, you can make predictions about your own life or about national, international, environmental, or scientific issues.

Example:

> It is likely that one day human life on Earth will be destroyed by a huge meteor.

Expressions	Examples
Highly probable Very probable Very likely	
Quite probable Quite likely Not unlikely Not improbable Very possible	
Probable More than possible Likely	
Possible Perhaps Maybe	

Exercise B

Switch your sentences with your partner and ask your partner questions about his or her predictions. You can agree or disagree with and discuss each other's predictions.

Idiomatic and Fixed Expressions

The following expressions and idioms are related to the subject of possibility, probability, and certainty.

In teams of two, read the examples and guess each expression's degree of certainty. You can use percentages (100 percent, 80 percent, etc.) or words (*certain*, *probable*, *possible*, *likely*, *impossible*, etc.). Check your dictionary if necessary.

Expression	Degree of certainty	Example
For sure		If the government doesn't help at-risk businesses, many of them will go bankrupt for sure.
A safe bet		If you want a good defence lawyer, mine is a safe bet.
Not to stand a chance (to)		He thinks he is going to win this case, but he doesn't stand a chance.
Not to rule out		Despite the new security measures, I'm afraid we still cannot rule out future terrorist attacks.
Not to be out of the question		Despite his lawyer's efforts, a second-degree murder charge is not out of the question yet.
Once in a blue moon		I only see my brother once in a blue moon, but we call each other regularly.
Not to bank on something		I hope you get the loan, but don't bank on it yet.
To be in the cards		I think a federal election might be in the cards early next year.

Canadian Outlook

Homicide Rates in Canada

Table 1 below compares the homicide rate of all the countries in the Americas. As you can see, Canada and Bermuda have the lowest rates in this part of the world.

Table 2 shows the homicide rates in the OECD (Organisation for Economic Co-operation and Development) countries. As you can see, except for Mexico, the United States, Turkey, and South Korea, the murder rate in all OECD countries is under 2 percent.

1. Based on your own experience and what you read in this chapter, discuss what elements cause the homicide rates in some countries to be high and in others to be low.
2. The murder rate in Japan is at 0.4 per 100,000. How do you think Japan has been able to achieve such a low rate?

Table 1: Homicide rate per 100,000 population, Americas region, by country (criminal justice, latest available year; public health, 2004)

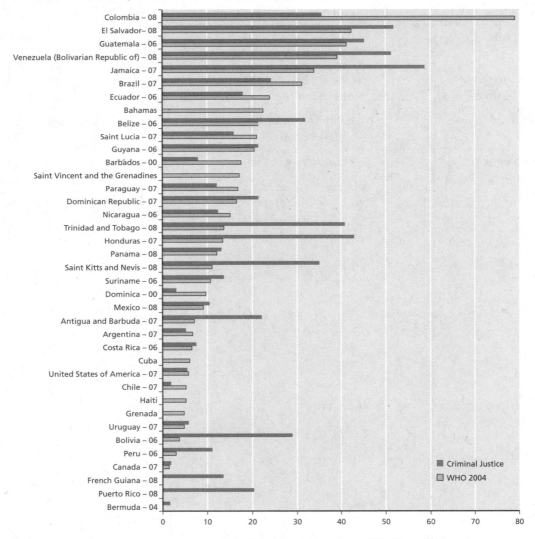

Intentional homicide rate per 100,000 population

Table 2: Homicide rates in the OECD countries

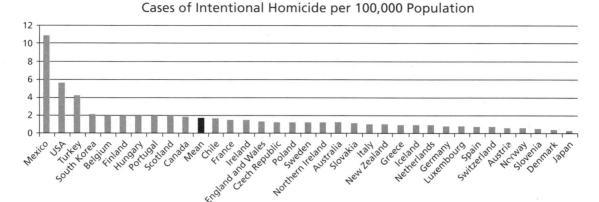

Cases of Intentional Homicide per 100,000 Population

Writing

Supporting Topic Sentences

The introduction, conclusion, and the topic sentences in the following essay have been provided for you. Develop each of the three body paragraphs by clarifying and developing their topic sentences.

Say No to Capital Punishment

Although the death penalty has been abolished in most countries in the world as an inhuman practice, there are still 58 nations that use capital punishment as a legal sentence for a range of different crimes. Some of these countries are dictatorships that execute even minors while others are democracies where lesser punishments such as torture have been illegal for a long time. How could such countries continue to execute? It's about time all humanity stopped this barbaric and cruel punishment.

Many people support capital punishment as an act of revenge. They believe in an eye-for-an-eye philosophy. One has to ask such people, "What is the difference between a murderer who kills for vengeance and the government that kills the murderer for revenge?" _____

_____

_____

Another group of supporters believes that fear of capital punishment will make murderers think twice before committing murder. This is a false belief because _____

_____

_____

_____

Another common reason for capital punishment is cost. Some supporters, mostly among politicians, believe that keeping a criminal in prison for life is costly. It is basically cheaper to kill. In answer to this group _____

_____

_____

As shown in this essay, capital punishment is not only inhuman but also illogical. Governments should not be agents of revenge. Moreover, the death penalty is neither a deterrent nor economical. Crime can only be reduced by addressing social injustice, removing poverty, and educating the public.

Chapter 9

Cosmic Collision

Introduction

Our Solar System

Pair work: How many of the 10 objects in the picture of our solar system can you name?

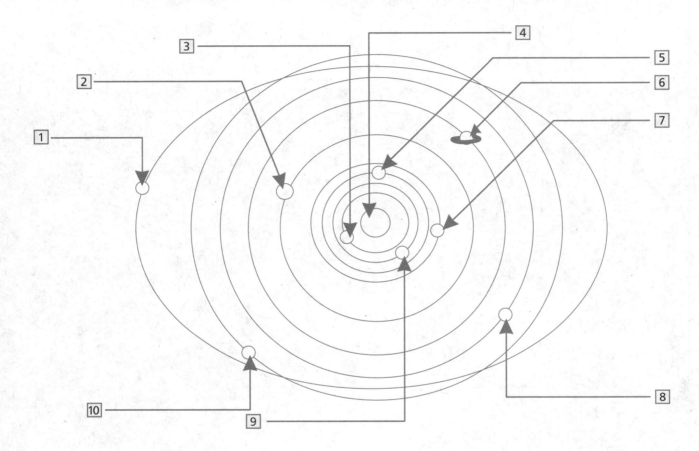

Can you define the following words?

   galaxy
   star
   planet
   satellite (moon)
   asteroid
   comet
   dwarf planet
   orbit

Reading

Warm-Up Questions

1. How old is the universe?
2. How old is Earth?
3. How old is humankind?

Vocabulary

Read the definitions below and find the word from the reading passage that corresponds to each definition. To help you, the first and the last letter of each word are provided.

Unbelievably	I	Y
A person who studies the stars and the universe	A	R
Very large; huge	G	C
To move around quickly in a circle	S	L
To go in a circle around a central point	R	E
To become greater in size	E	D
To move quickly away from a surface hit; to be reflected	B	E
Brought together to form a tight group	C	D
A thick, flat slice or piece of something	S	B
An idea or explanation of something that is based on a few known facts, but that has not yet been proved to be true or correct	H	S
A very large rock that has been shaped by water or the weather	B	R
A part of something that is left after the other parts have been used, removed, destroyed	R	T
A thick solid piece that has been broken off something	C	K
Not clear in shape; covered with short soft fine hair or fur	F	Y

Our Universe

No one knows how big the universe is. Astronomers believe that it is still growing outward in every direction. How did it all begin? No one knows that for sure either.

Most scientists believe that at first everything was one incredibly solid, heavy ball of matter. This ball exploded about 13.7 billion years ago—and the universe was born. The moment of this explosion is called the "big bang." It is from this moment that time began.

After the explosion, the early universe was small and extremely hot. As it cooled, it expanded and pieces spread out. Small pieces formed the basic elements hydrogen and helium. Other pieces began to join together, and objects began to form. Over billions of years the objects became galaxies, stars, and planets.

Billions of years ago our solar system was nothing but a gigantic swirling cloud of gas and dust. This cloud packed together and became extremely hot. Eventually, the centre of the cloud formed our sun about 4.57 billion years ago. The rest of the cloud clumped together until it formed the planets. Eight planets in our solar system revolve around our sun. Beginning with the one closest to the sun, they are Mercury, Venus, Earth, Mars, Jupiter, Saturn, Uranus, and Neptune.

The planets have been divided into two basic groups. There are Earth-like planets and Jupiter-like planets. Earth-like planets are close to the sun in an area called the inner solar system and are made up of rock and metal. These planets are Mercury, Venus, Earth, and Mars. The outer solar system planets are larger and farther away from the sun. These planets are Jupiter, Saturn, Uranus, and Neptune. These four planets have no solid surfaces. They are made up of gases and liquids.

There are also thousands of asteroids in our solar system. They tend to vary in shape, ranging from large spheres to smaller slabs and potato-shaped objects. Some asteroids are big. Most are the size of a boulder. Smaller asteroids form when two big asteroids smash into each other and break up. Astronomers think that there are millions of tiny asteroids in the solar system. Like planets, all asteroids in our solar system circle the sun. The path that a planet or an asteroid follows when it circles the sun is called an orbit. Most asteroids are found farther from the sun than Earth, in the asteroid belt between the orbits of Mars and Jupiter. Some, though, come quite close to the sun.

Scientists used to count an object called Pluto as another planet. But Pluto is neither Earth-like nor Jupiter-like. It is very small and frozen. So scientists now call Pluto a dwarf planet. Pluto is in a wide region of the solar system called the Kuiper belt, which is filled with other dwarf planets like Pluto, as well as smaller frozen remnants of the solar system's formation.

Another type of object often found in our solar system is a comet. Comets sometimes look like stars with hairy tails, but they are not stars. Like the moon, a comet has no light of its own. A comet shines from the sunlight bouncing off it. Like Earth, a comet goes around the sun, so it may appear again and again. But if a comet isn't a star, what is it? Some scientists think that a large part of a comet is ice. The rest is bits of iron and dust and perhaps a few big chunks of rock. When sunshine melts the ice in a comet, great clouds of gas go streaming behind it. These clouds make the bright fuzzy-looking tail.

Astronomers do not know how far out our solar system extends. They think that some objects may be as much as 9 trillion miles away from the sun in a far area of the solar system called the Oort cloud, but this is still a hypothesis. There's still a lot to be discovered about our solar system.

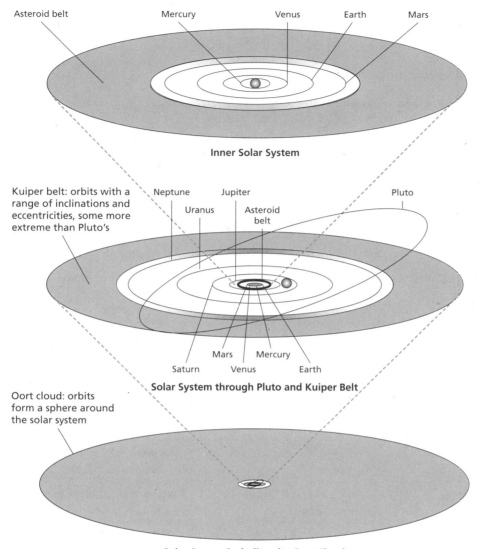

Inner Solar System

Asteroid belt   Mercury   Venus   Earth   Mars

Kuiper belt: orbits with a range of inclinations and eccentricities, some more extreme than Pluto's

Neptune   Jupiter   Pluto
Uranus   Asteroid belt

Saturn   Mars   Mercury   Earth
Venus

Solar System through Pluto and Kuiper Belt

Oort cloud: orbits form a sphere around the solar system

Solar System including the Oort Cloud

Comprehension

1. According to this passage, how many years ago did time begin?

2. Why do you think the theory that explains the beginning of the universe is called the "big bang"?

3. What were the first two chemical elements that were created?

4. Approximately how many years after the big bang was our sun formed?

5. What is the farthest planet from the sun?

6. What is the name of the area in the solar system where Earth-like planets are located?

7. What are Earth-like planets made of?

8. What are Jupiter-like planets made of?

9. What is the definition of an orbit?

10. How are the smaller asteroids formed?

11. What are dwarf planets made of?

12. Why does a comet shine?

13. What are the four components of a comet?

14. How far from the sun are some of the objects in the Oort cloud?

Grammar: Future Tenses

There are several different ways of expressing the future in English. Here are some of the most common ways:

Will (simple future)	Facts about the future, promises, prediction, instant decisions	The sun **will become** a red giant and will expand beyond Earth's orbit in about one to two billion years.
To be going to	Intention, prediction	Astronomers believe that a large asteroid **is going to hit** Earth sometime in the next 200,000 years.
Present progressive	Plans or arrangements in the future	I'm **meeting** a famous scientist at the conference tonight.
Simple present	Talking about a timetable or time schedule	The space shuttle **takes off** in exactly two hours.
Be to	Official arrangement (example a) A rule or an order (example b)	a) The president **is to visit** NASA's headquarters in April. b) During the president's visit, all security personnel **are to stay** alert.
Be about to	Near future	The shuttle **is about to take** off.
Will be + verb + *-ing* (future progressive)	Action at a specific time or timeframe in the future	This time next week, I **will be attending** a seminar on space tourism.
Will have + past participle (future perfect)	Something that is finished or completed by a certain time in the future	I hope by the time the next big asteroid approaches Earth, scientists **will have found** an effective way to destroy it before it hits Earth.
May, might, could	Possibility or probability in the future	See chapter 8 for examples
Aim / expect / hope / intend / plan + infinitive	Each verb adds its own meaning to future actions or events	I **hope / expect to pass** this course at the end of the semester. Scientists are **planning to send** humans to Mars by the year 2030.

Exercise A

Read each of the following situations. Use the verb *to be going to* to predict what each person intends to do next. There might be more than one correct answer.

Example:

Mary is hungry. She has just made a sandwich for herself. She _is going to eat it_.

1. The car approaches the intersection. The driver turns on the left signal.
   She _____ .

2. A car just hit a young boy. Amita saw the accident. She is taking her cellphone out of her pocket.
   She _____ .

3. Miranda is speeding. There is a police officer behind a tree with a radar speed gun pointed at her car. He _____ .

4. The tail of the fighter jet caught fire. The jet is going down. The pilot is putting on his parachute.
   He _____ .

5. A boy is busy blowing up a balloon. His sister is hiding behind him with a needle is her hand.
   She _____ .

6. Kanda and her husband are waiting at the bus stop. A bus is approaching.
   They _____ .

7. Alan is afraid of cats. Alicia's cat just jumped on his lap.
   Alan _____ .

Exercise B

Fill in the blanks using simple (e.g., *will do*), progressive (e.g., *will be doing*), or perfect future (e.g., *will have done*). There might be more than one correct answer for some of the blanks.

1. We know that an asteroid _____ (hit) Earth. We just don't know when.

2. Scientists are sure they _____ (discover) a cure for cancer by the end of the century.

3. If I get the admission letter, I _____ (study) space science at York University at this time next year.

4. If you are interested in astronomy, you should read Stephen Hawking's books.
   They _____ (change) your life.

5. I _____ (visit) Professor Backman this afternoon.

6. I don't know much about astrophysics, but if I read as much as I'm reading now,
   I _____ (learn) most of the basics by the end of the year.

7. _____ you _____ (pass) by the library today? I have some books I was hoping you could return for me.

Grammar Reinforcement

Choose the best answer.

1. I wrote the test but I'm not sure about the result. I _____ pass.
   a) will
   b) might
   c) am going to

2. Cellphones are not allowed during the exam. All students _____ leave their cellphones in their lockers before entering class.
   a) are to
   b) will
   c) are about to

3. The plane _____ on time, at 3:30.
   a) is about to arrive
   b) arrives
   c) plans to arrive

4. He has put so much air into the balloon that it _____ .
   a) is to burst
   b) is about to burst
   c) bursts

5. I studied very hard for yesterday's test. I _____ to pass.
   a) expect
   b) intend
   c) plan

6. I _____ to get married and have kids someday.
   a) aim
   b) am about to
   c) hope

7. What _____ this weekend? Will you go to the movies with me?
   a) do you do
   b) are you doing
   c) are you to do

8. Help me please! I _____ !
   a) will fall
   b) am going to fall
   c) fall

9. Do you need a ride? No, thanks! George _____ a ride home.
   a) is giving me
   b) gives me
   c) may give me

10. When he retires next week, Dr. Naderi _____ for NASA for 35 years.
    a) will work
    b) will be working
    c) will have worked

The Film: *Cosmic Collision*

Video Vocabulary

The following words and expressions are used in the video. Study them before watching.

Celestial	Related to the sky; not related to the earth
Cosmic	Connected with the universe; very big and important
Collision	An accident in which two moving objects or people crash into each other
Encounter	A meeting (especially a frightening one)
Impact	The act of one object hitting another; the force with which an object hits another
Scar	A mark that is left on the skin after a wound has healed; mark left after impact
Fragment	A small part of something that has broken off or comes from something larger
Catastrophe	A terrible event that causes a lot of destruction and suffering; a disaster
Hazard	A thing that can be dangerous or cause damage; a threat; a danger
Crater	A large hole in the ground caused by something large hitting it
Observatory	A special building from which scientists watch the stars
Species	A group of animals or plants whose members are similar
Detonate	To make a bomb or other device explode
Tectonic plates	Large sheets of rock that form the earth's surface
Decade	10 Years
Century	100 Years
Millennium	1000 Years

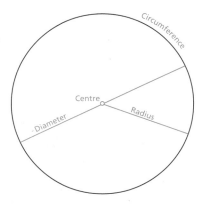

Warm-Up Questions

1. When you look at the moon at night, you can see lots of dark spots. What do you think they are?
2. What do you think we can do if a big asteroid or comet heads for Earth? Is there any way to prevent it from hitting us?

Comprehension

Exercise A

The clip you are going to watch is about the possibility of a large asteroid or comet impact with Earth. Watch it once. First match the names of the people with their position or places they work (see chart below), and then match their names with the statements in the chart. The first one has been done for you as an example.

1. Catherine Fol
   Position: _b_
   Statement: _I_

2. Robert Jedicke
   Position: ____
   Statement: ____

3. Eugene Shoemaker
   Position: ____
   Statement: ____

4. George Coyne
   Position: ____
   Statement: ____

5. David Morrison
   Position: ____
   Statement: ____

Position	Statement
a) US Geological Survey b) Narrator & film director c) Director of Vatican observatory d) NASA Ames Research Center e) University of Arizona Lunar and Planetary Laboratory	I. The moon and Earth are side by side so their surfaces should look similar, but Earth's scars are less apparent than the moon's because life on Earth is stronger. II. The human species, like other species, is due to become extinct. Species come and go. III. A large cosmic collision is a low probability event with terrible consequences. IV. I believe all the water necessary for life on Earth was brought by comets, and the elements necessary for organic compounds were delivered by comets. V. We find about 2000 new asteroids per month but only 3 or 4 of them are near-Earth asteroids.

Exercise B

Watch the clip one more time and circle *T* if the statement is true or *F* if it is false. Also correct the false statements.

1. The comet Shoemaker-Levy hit Jupiter in the summer of 1984.   T   F
2. There have been several records of people killed because a meteorite hit them.   T   F
3. The Tunguska impact in Siberia happened in 1980.   T   F
4. The Tunguska asteroid was 60 metres across.   T   F
5. There are at least 140 impact craters on Earth.   T   F
6. The Manicouagan Reservoir is an impact crater located in Quebec, Canada.   T   F
7. The Manicouagan Reservoir is one-sixteenth the size of the island of Montreal.   T   F
8. The asteroid belt is located between the orbits of Earth and Mars.   T   F
9. Both the Oort cloud and the Kuiper belt contain comets.   T   F
10. The impact that killed off the dinosaurs happened 85 million years ago.   T   F

11. The impact that killed off the dinosaurs happened in the Gulf of Mexico.   T   F

12. In five billion years, the sun will become cold and die out.   T   F

13. None of the known large objects in space is a danger to Earth, at least in the next several centuries.   T   F

14. Less than 10 percent of the asteroids and comets have been discovered.   T   F

15. We have the technology to stop asteroids from hitting Earth if we have enough warning.   T   F

16. There are a few hours from the time an asteroid enters the atmosphere until it explodes on the ground.   T   F

17. When it comes to survival and adaptation, humans are superior to insects.   T   F

18. Asteroid and comet impacts are normal, natural events and part of evolution.   T   F

Writing

In this chapter you saw one theory about how life on Earth will end (cosmic collision). Think about all the other possible ways life on Earth could be destroyed. Choose one as the most likely way and write a paragraph about how and when you think life on Earth will end.

Reading

Vocabulary

Read the sentences below and guess the meaning of the words in bold. You can also see the words in context in the following passage. Then check your dictionary to see if you guessed the meaning correctly.

1. The force of friction slowed the shuttle down as it re-entered the earth's atmosphere.

2. It is sometimes difficult to draw a distinction between a planet and a dwarf planet.

3. As the bomb fell over Hiroshima and exploded, the entire city disappeared.

4. He deposited a pile of books on my desk.

5. The weather report forecast snow for tomorrow.

6. Lottery numbers are usually chosen at random by a computer.

7. Several people were injured in the bomb blast.

8. The chimney toppled down in the earthquake.

9. Canada **dispatched** troops to Afghanistan.

10. *Spirit* and *Opportunity* are two famous **space probes** sent to Mars in 2003.

11. The dishwasher was too heavy to lift, so I **nudged** it into place with my knee.

12. When there is heavy traffic on the highway, I use another **route**.

13. Police arrested the person responsible for putting the computer virus **in circulation**.

14. Insects can easily **cope with** extreme conditions; humans can't.

Warm-Up Questions

1. Have you ever seen a crater?
2. What do you think can cause a crater besides cosmic collisions?

Cosmic Collisions

Anyone who watches the sky on a dark, clear night (not so easy with all the light pollution nowadays) will see the occasional flashes of shooting stars. These—more accurately known as meteors—are small dust particles which Earth sweeps up as it moves round the sun. Like all objects in the inner solar system, they are moving with speeds measured in kilometres per second. When they hit Earth's atmosphere, the **friction** produced by such speeds heats the dust particles until they burn up completely. The flash of a shooting star signals its end.

A **distinction** is usually **drawn** between a meteor, which does not reach the surface of Earth, and a meteorite, which does. To come through the **entire** atmosphere, a meteorite (usually a comet or an asteroid in origin) must be much larger than a dust particle. It has to be able to burn off its outer layers on the way down, and still have enough left to **deposit** material on the surface. Meteorites are quite capable of depositing many kilograms of rocks, but they occur much more rarely than shooting stars. Typically, only a handful of meteorite falls are recorded each year. Their potential for landing on people's heads is therefore very limited. But the existence of meteorites raises an obvious question. Can we identify nearby objects and **forecast** a collision and prevent it from happening?

Impacts seem to occur **at random**, so it is not possible to attempt any precise forecasting. Still, the average rate derived by scientists suggests that an impact that will form a crater 10 kilometres in diameter should happen within the next 200,000 years or so. Such an impact will not have a globally disastrous effect—that requires bigger explosions. But it could still have a major local effect. As with bombs, the effect of an impact is not restricted to the area of the actual crater. The explosion makes the surrounding atmosphere expand rapidly, producing a **blast** wave that spreads over a much larger region. For example, if the incoming body were to hit a city such as New York or London, the crater formed would only destroy part of the city. But the blast produced would **topple** buildings throughout the whole of the city and some way beyond. This blast effect is more important from our human viewpoint than the crater itself.

Supposing that a potential Earth collider can be identified, there still remains the question of what to do about it. The currently favoured option is to **dispatch** a **space probe** to the oncoming object, and use rockets on the probe to **nudge** the fragment into a safer orbit. How this might be done depends on the physical nature of the object. Some are solid objects that can be pushed or pulled. Others are weakly bound fragments that would easily fall to pieces. In some cases, the only **route** might be to blow the object up entirely, so that should any fragments hit Earth they would be too small to produce big craters. These are the thoughts in circulation today. We can hope that our descendants will be a good deal cleverer than we are, and will come up with better solutions.

In the long term as human beings count it, but in the short term on an astronomical timescale, the next major impact will occur. We can always hope that by then our descendants will have found methods of coping with it. To do that will require a detailed knowledge of the impacting bodies—where they come from and what they are like.

Comprehension

1. What is a meteor (shooting star)?

2. Why do meteors burn when they enter Earth's atmosphere?

3. What is the difference between a meteor and a meteorite?

4. Why are meteorites rarer than shooting stars?

5. Why is it difficult to predict the exact time of meteorite impacts?

6. Using an example, show how the blast wave is more dangerous than the impact itself.

7. Based on current science, what are the two best ways to stop an Earth collider?

8. Why is detailed knowledge of impacting bodies necessary for humans?

Listening

Vocabulary

Infrared	Electromagnetic waves that are longer than those of red light in the spectrum, and which cannot be seen
Dual	Having two parts or aspects; twin; double
Astronomical unit (AU)	A unit of measurement equal to 149.6 million kilometres, which is the distance from the centre of Earth to the sun
To shepherd	To guide somebody or something somewhere, making sure they go where you want them to go; to control
Spectrometer	A piece of equipment for measuring the wavelengths of coloured light
Alien civilization	Intelligent civilizations from other planets
To confine	To keep somebody or something inside the limits of a particular activity, subject, area, etc.

Warm-Up Questions

1. Have you ever watched the *Star Trek* series on TV?
2. Do you think there are other solar systems similar to ours?
3. Do you believe there is intelligent life somewhere in the universe besides Earth?

Epsilon Eridani

Exercise A

The star Epsilon Eridani is even stranger than fiction. NASA's Spitzer space telescope has shown another strange fact about this star system.

Listen to the audio and fill in the blanks with the missing words. Pay attention to your spelling.

Twin Asteroid Belts

It's one of the proposed locations for *Star Trek*'s planet Vulcan. It was the location of space station *Babylon 5* in the popular '90s television 1_____ It has been featured in novels by Isaac Asimov and Frank Herbert. But the star Epsilon Eridani is even 2_____ than fiction. NASA's Spitzer space telescope has shown it has *two* asteroid belts. Hello, I'm Daniel Brennan.

This Spitzer space telescope podcast is part of a series highlighting recent discoveries in infrared 3_____. It's produced by NASA's Spitzer Science Center at the California Institute of Technology in Pasadena. The Spitzer 4_____ is managed by NASA's Jet Propulsion Laboratory.

Epsilon Eridani is a star much like our own sun, but younger and slightly 5_____. It has the distinction of being the closest known 6_____ system to our own. Astronomers had previously found evidence for two possible planets in the system and a broad, outer ring of icy 7_____ much like our own Kuiper belt.

Now, Spitzer has discovered that the system also has dual asteroid belts. Our own solar system has just one, between the orbits of 8_____ and Jupiter at a distance of 3 AU from the sun. In the Epsilon Eridani system, the first belt sits approximately this same 9_____ out from the central star, and the second one lies between the first belt and the comet ring, at about 20 AU. That would be the equivalent of an asteroid belt slightly 10_____ the orbit of Uranus.

Except for the mysterious second asteroid belt, the Epsilon Eridani system is an excellent analog for our own solar system when life first 11_____ on Earth, according to Dr. Dana Backman of the SETI Institute in Mountain View, California, the lead author of a paper about the findings set to appear in the January 10, 2009, edition of the *Astrophysical* 12_____.

Asteroid belts are rocky and metallic debris left over from the early stages of planet formation. Their presence around other stars signals that rocky planets like Earth could be 13_____ in the system's inner regions, with 14_____ gas planets circling near the belts' 15_____. In our own solar system, for example, there is evidence that Jupiter, which lies beyond our asteroid belt, caused the asteroid belt to form long ago by stirring up material that otherwise would have coalesced into a planet. Nowadays, Jupiter's 16_____ shepherds the asteroid belt, keeping it confined to a 17_____.

The presence of two asteroid belts indicates that there might be additional planets beyond the two already discovered. These 18_____ planets could be lying unobserved between the orbits of the other two, shepherding material around Epsilon Eridani.

Astronomers have detected stars with signs of 19_____ belts of material before, but Epsilon Eridani is closer to the earth and more like our sun overall. It's a mere 10 light years away, slightly less 20_____ than the sun, and roughly 800 million years old.

Spitzer observed Epsilon Eridani with both its infrared cameras and its infrared spectrometer. When asteroids and comets collide or evaporate, they release tiny 21_____ of dust that give off heat, which Spitzer can see. Because the system is so close to us, Spitzer can detect the dust more easily than it can around more 22_____ stars, allowing us to form a more detailed understanding of the system's architecture.

Epsilon Eridani was one of the first stars searched for signs of 23 _____ alien civilization using radio telescopes in 1960. At that time, astronomers did not know how young the star is. But whether in science or science fiction, Epsilon Eridani is 24 _____ another example of how much more we still have to learn about the stars. For the Spitzer Science Center, I'm Daniel Brennan.

Exercise B

Listen to the program a second time and answer the following questions.

1. What are two differences between Epsilon Eridani and our sun?

2. What does the existence of the second asteroid belt mean for astronomers?

3. Provide the following information about Epsilon Eridani:

   Epsilon Eridani's age: _____ years old

   Epsilon Eridani's distance from Earth: _____ light years

   The central star's distance from the first asteroid belt: _____ AU

   The central star's distance from the second asteroid belt: _____ AU

Speaking

Discussing the End of Civilization

The table below shows you some possible events that may cause the extinction of the human species. In teams of two, discuss the following questions. Try to use the future forms you have learned in this chapter as much as possible.

- What will happen at different stages of this event?
- Are some people going to survive?
- How might we prevent this event? What are the steps we need to take in the near future to make sure this won't happen?

Doomsday Scenario	Example
Cosmic collisions	Asteroid or comet impacts
Omnicide	Humans killing humans: nuclear war, biological war, etc.
Human-made biological catastrophe	Global warming
Alien invasion	A species from another planet attacking Earth
Ice age	A drop in temperatures on Earth
Ecological disasters	Large-scale volcanism, drought, famine, massive earthquakes, mega-tsunamis, etc.
Pandemic	A highly contagious killer disease involving large populations
Solar flare	Sudden explosions or flares of energy on the sun's surface creating extreme heat
Robot takeover	Human-made intelligent machines destroying humans

Can you think of any other scenarios that might end human life on Earth?

Idiomatic and Fixed Expressions

The following expressions and idioms are related to astronomical bodies. Read the examples and fill in the blanks with the following words. You might use some of the words more than once.

moon	sun	stars	planet

Then in teams of two or three guess the meaning of each expression. Check your dictionaries to see if you guessed correctly.

Expression	Example
Be (living) on another . . .	The prime minister says the tax increase won't affect families. I wonder what _____ he is on!
Ask/cry for the . . .	I asked my boss for two days off. He looked at me as if I was asking for the _____.
Hitch your wagon to a . . .	He is such a successful man. If I were you, I'd hitch my wagon to that _____.
A/somebody's place in the . . .	After struggling for years to make a name for myself, I finally earned my place in the _____.
Thank/bless one's lucky . . .	I lost my wallet when my plane landed in Canada. I thank my lucky _____ I didn't lose it when I was overseas.
Under the . . .	He pretends to know everything under the _____.
Promise (somebody) the	When they were going to employ me, they promised me the _____, but later broke all their promises.
Reach for the . . .	My mom always wanted me to reach for the _____, but I wasn't ambitious enough, I guess.
It's written in the . . .	Those two were made for each other. Their marriage was written in the _____
Once in a blue . . .	I don't see my brother very often. I see him only once in a blue _____.
. . .-crossed lovers	*Romeo and Juliet* is the story of two _____-crossed lovers.
Be over the . . .	Charles finally received his admission letter from the university. You should see how happy he is. He is over the _____!

Canadian Outlook

Canada in Space

Canadians have contributed to astronomy and space exploration in important ways. The table below consists of names of Canadian scientists, astronauts, and space machinery. How many of the names have you heard before? Choose one name and research its background. Bring your research results to class.

Astronauts	Scientists	Machines
Marc Garneau	Gilles Fontaine	Canadarm
Roberta Bondar	Werner Israel	Alouette
Chris Hadfield	James Chamberlin	the Anik series
Julie Payette	Owen Maynard	RADARSAT

Writing

Predicting Future Trends

Select two of the categories from the box below. Write one paragraph for each about what trend or trends you predict will emerge 25 years from now in the categories you have chosen. Support your predictions with reasons and examples.

transportation	space travel	communication
home building	government	medicine

Example:

Economy

Twenty-five years from now, we will live in a cashless society. There will no longer be any actual money or even plastic credit cards because technology will have found a more efficient way to pay for purchases. All people will have microchips under their skin that businesses will scan to get their money, or they might use biometric scans, such as fingerprint or retina scans, to take money from the customer's account. This is going to happen because in a cashless society, there will be fewer crimes and counterfeiting. Also, fewer people will be able to cheat on their taxes. Governments and banks will win. People, though, will lose because they will have almost no privacy and they will pay more commissions to banks and corporations. However, people will easily give up their rights in exchange for convenience and discounts, much the same way they are doing these days on the Internet.

Chapter 10

Tagged

STUDIO

Introduction

Online Privacy Survey

Answer the following yes/no questions about your online habits. Circle your answers.

1.	Do you post personal or family photos on social-networking sites such as Facebook?	Yes	No
2.	Have you ever posted your complete birth date on social-networking sites?	Yes	No
3.	Do you put status and location updates on sites such as Facebook Places or Foursquare?	Yes	No
4.	Have you ever posted your home address or telephone number online?	Yes	No
5.	Have you ever shared your likes and dislikes (such as books, movies, music, brands, etc.) online?	Yes	No
6.	Do you do your banking online?	Yes	No
7.	Have you ever logged into your personal accounts (email, Facebook, bank account, etc.) on a public network at places such as coffee shops and airports?	Yes	No
8.	Have you ever sent sensitive information such as credit-card numbers and banking information in an email?	Yes	No
9.	Do you use simple passwords consisting of words and numbers only?	Yes	No
10.	Do you use the same password for several accounts?	Yes	No

How many *yes* answers do you have? Do you think you are careful or careless with your online security and privacy? Now compare your answers to those of other students in class. Which question has the highest number of *no* answers in class?

Reading

Warm-Up Questions

1. How do you define *privacy*?
2. Do you believe privacy is less important in modern times?

Vocabulary

Exercise A

Match the verbs on the left with their meanings on the right.

1. ____ Resolve	a)	Reject or refuse to consider an offer, a proposal, etc. or the person who makes it
2. ____ Threaten	b)	Get information in order to decide whether someone is appropriate for something; for example, a job, immigration, etc.
3. ____ Justify		
4. ____ Turn down		
5. ____ Monitor	c)	Check something or watch someone regularly in order to find out what is happening
6. ____ Compromise	d)	Find an acceptable solution to a problem
7. ____ Deter	e)	Be greater or more important than something
8. ____ Outweigh	f)	Give an explanation or excuse for something or for doing something
9. ____ Screen		
	g)	Be a danger to; to be likely to harm or destroy something
	h)	Give up some of your demands after a disagreement with somebody in order to reach an agreement
	i)	Try to prevent; to show opposition to

Exercise B

Match the nouns and adjectives on the left with their meanings on the right.

1. ____ Controversial	a)	Using measurements of human features, such as fingers or eyes, in order to identify people
2. ____ Consumer	b)	A person who secretly finds a way of looking at or changing information on somebody else's computer system without permission
3. ____ Goods		
4. ____ Spammer		
5. ____ Hacker	c)	A person who sends mail, especially advertising material, through the internet to a large number of people who have not asked for it
6. ____ Predator	d)	The act of carefully watching a person suspected of a crime or a place where a crime may be committed
7. ____ Anonymity		
8. ____ Vulnerable	e)	Things that are produced to be sold
9. ____ Whistleblower	f)	Causing a lot of angry public discussion and disagreement
10. ____ Biometric	g)	A person or an organization that uses weaker people for their own advantage
11. ____ Surveillance	h)	The state of remaining unknown to most other people
	i)	Easy to attack and hurt
	j)	A person who informs people in authority or the public that the company they work for is doing something wrong or illegal
	k)	A person who buys things or uses services

Privacy Issues

As important as the right of privacy is to so many people, it is clearly not the only consideration in making decisions about how society will be organized. What makes privacy issues so often controversial and hard to resolve is the conflict between privacy and other important goals, such as business efficiency, law enforcement, and, particularly in recent years, fighting terrorism. Because hardly anyone is against privacy by itself, privacy issues generally involve one side saying that privacy is being threatened and the other side saying that the threat is minimal and is justified by important social, commercial, or governmental interests.

Privacy issues are found in almost every activity and institution of modern life. Today some of the most important ones include:

- What should happen to the information consumers provide when they buy something in a store or online?
- Is it acceptable for websites to track users if it enables them to provide a more "personalized" and relevant selection of goods?
- Should companies have to ask permission before they distribute customer information—or is it up to the customer to say no?
- If information can be collected only if the consumer allows it, will the availability of credit and other services decline, and costs go up?
- Who should have access to a person's medical information? Should insurers be allowed to turn down persons who have genetic risks of disease? What role, if any, should medical records play in employment decisions?
- Should employee use of email, chat rooms, and websites be monitored to avoid potential lawsuits?
- How can children be given access to the rich resources of the Internet without compromising their or their family's privacy?
- Should all email and other Internet activity be digitally traceable? Would the ability to find and punish spammers, hackers, or online predators outweigh the loss of anonymity that might protect vulnerable people or whistleblowers?
- Would the use of a universal ID card, biometric passports, airline passenger screening, and integrated databases make the nation safer from terrorism? If so, would it be worth the cost in privacy and the ability to move freely without having to be accountable to a largely unseen and unknown security system?
- Is it a good idea to have surveillance cameras in major public places? Does it not only deter crime but also deter people from associating freely? Should any restrictions be placed on web cams and camera phones that allow anyone to capture images?
- Are we becoming a "surveillance society"? Should we admit that privacy is a lost cause, or give people the technical and legal tools to "watch the watchers"?

Comprehension

1. What makes privacy issues controversial?

2. Give examples of some goals that might conflict with privacy.

3. In teams of two or three choose four of the questions in the reading passage above. Then discuss and try to find answers to those questions. Share the results of your discussions with the rest of your class.

Grammar: Question Formation Review

Different Purposes of Questions

We might ask questions for different purposes. The table below shows some of these purposes.

	Purpose	Example	Meaning
A	To get information	Are you home? When will you be home?	The speaker wants information about somebody's presence or the time of their presence.
B	To start a conversation	Isn't it lovely today? Did you watch the hockey game last night?	The speaker wants to start a conversation. He or she probably already knows the answers.
C	To give a comment	Did you check your dictionary when you wrote this essay?	The speaker really means that the essay is full of spelling mistakes.
D	To check knowledge	Teacher: What city is the capital of Canada?	The teacher wants to check the knowledge of the students. He or she already knows the answer.
E	To give an order or make a polite request (mostly with modals)	Will you close the door? Could you show me the way?	The speaker expects the other person to do something.
F	To ask for permission (mostly with modals)	Could I borrow your pen? May I use your phone?	The speaker wants to get the other person's permission.
G	To make an invitation or an offering (mostly with modals)	Would you like to go to the movies with me? Can I help you with your books?	The speaker is inviting the other person to the movies or offering help.

Exercise A

Use the letters (*A, B, C, D*, etc.) from the table above to identify the purpose of the following questions.

1. (To your roommate): Will you shut up? _____
2. (To your roommate): Would you like to come with me for a cup of coffee? _____
3. (Teacher to student): What is the meaning of the word *predator*? _____
4. (Student to teacher): What is the meaning of the word *predator*? _____
5. (Student to teacher): May I go to the washroom? _____
6. (Teacher to student): Did you use the grammar-check feature on your computer before handing in your homework? _____
7. (Man on elevator to stranger): Aren't these elevators slow? _____

Form

Yes/no questions are questions that are answered with *yes* or *no* (see examples in the Online Privacy Survey on page 177).

To form a yes/no question, we use the following formula:

auxiliary + subject + verb (ASV)

Examples:

He is studying. → Is he studying?
S A   V   A S   V

I can help you. → Can I help you?

He has gone. → Has he gone?

Note: If there is more than one auxiliary verb in the sentence, only the first auxiliary verb moves before the verb.

He could have gone there. → Could he have gone there?
    A1 A2 V   A1   A2 V

List of the most common auxiliary verbs in English:

am	did	should
is	have	can
are	has	could
was	had	may
were	will	might
do	would	must
does	shall	ought to

When there is no auxiliary verb in the sentence (as in simple past and simple present of most verbs), we have to add the auxiliaries *do*, *does*, or *did*. (See Chapters 1 and 3 for more examples).

Examples:

He goes home. → Does he go home?

They go home. → Do they go home?

He went home. → Did he go home?

Exercise B

Change the following sentences to yes/no questions.

1. He has chosen a good password for his account.

2. He leaves his USB drive on my computer every time.

3. She will send you an SMS soon.

4. Spammers send a lot of junk mail to my inbox.

5. They should protect their privacy.

6. I lost all the information on my hard drive.

7. They had warned you about this computer virus before.

8. She should have monitored her email.

9. He has been using Facebook for several years.

10. The antivirus program was running in the background.

WH-questions (information questions) are questions that start with a question word (such as *what*, *when*, *where*, etc.). It is not possible to answer yes or no to these questions.

To form a WH-question, we use the following formula:

question word + auxiliary + subject + verb (QASV)

Examples:

He is studying programming. → What is he studying?
S A   V   Q   A S   V

She could see you tonight. → When could she see you?

He came here on foot. → How did he come here?

These are the most common question words in English:

where	what	which
who(m)	why	how
when	whose	

Note: the question word *how* can be combined with several adjectives to form different questions. Here are some examples:

how much	how far	how high
how many	how tall	how wide
how often	how long	

Note: When asking a WH-question about the subject or part of the subject, the word order doesn't change. Read the following sentences.

Mike loves Joan. → Who does Mike love?

Mike loves Joan. → Who loves Joan?

In the first sentence the word order changes because the question is about Joan, the object. In the second sentence the word order doesn't change because the question is about Mike, the subject.

Exercise C

Change the following sentences to WH-questions. The underlined part is the answer and should be removed from the question.

1. Bill Gates and Paul Allen founded Microsoft in 1975.

2. This computer runs slowly because of a Trojan horse.

3. You can protect your information by setting a strong password.

4. They spend a lot of time on Facebook.

5. She has had her computer for three years.

6. I check my email six times a day.

7. I will borrow Trevor's computer for the weekend.

8. I bought this cellphone <u>in Moncton</u>.

9. Jennifer knows <u>Mark Zuckerberg</u>.

10. <u>Mark Zuckerberg</u> knows Jennifer.

Negative Questions

Negative questions are formed by adding *-n't* to the auxiliary verb.

> Should you? → Shouldn't you?
>
> Is he? → Isn't he?
>
> Do you? → Don't you?

Negative questions are used for several purposes including the following:

To show surprise	Haven't you done your homework yet? (I'm surprised that your homework is not done yet.)
To make the other person agree with you or when you expect the answer to be yes	Aren't you Tom's brother? (I'm pretty sure you are Tom's brother.)
To make a complaint or an impolite request (usually with modals)	Won't you shut up? (Shut up!) Can't you sit still? (Sit still!)
To make a suggestion or to criticise (usually with *why*)	Why don't we go to the movies? (Let's go to the movies.) Why didn't you do your homework? (You should have done your homework.)

Exercise D

Write negative questions for the following situations.

1. I'm pretty sure you are the person who helped me last time. (expect the answer to be yes)

2. It's better if you reset your computer. (suggest)

3. Wow! I can't believe you haven't changed your old computer yet. (surprise)

4. You should have changed your password. (criticize)

5. Keep quiet! (complain)

Grammar Reinforcement

Work in teams of two. One student asks questions based on each situation. The second student answers. The first student writes down the other student's answers and makes recommendations. Then they switch roles.

Situation 1: You are at a restaurant. One of you is a waiter and the other is a customer. The waiter asks questions. The customer answers and asks his or her own questions. You may use the clues below.

drinks → pop, wine, beer, or water
appetizer → soup or salad
>   soup types (onion soup, cream of broccoli, or chicken noodle)
>   salad (garden, Caesar, or mixed green)
>   salad dressing (Italian, Caesar, or vinaigrette)

main course → steak, pasta, or pizza

steak (rare, medium, or well done; 8, 10, or 12 oz)

pasta (spaghetti and meatballs, linguini, or fettuccine alfredo)

pizza (thin or thick crust; chicken, veggie, shrimp, beef, or pepperoni)

dessert → coffee (black, milk, cream, or sugar)

chocolate cake, cheesecake, banana split, or apple pie

Situation 2: You want to buy a new laptop. One of you is the sales rep and the other is a customer. The sales rep asks questions and makes suggestions. The customer answers. You may use the following suggestions.

purpose → gaming, business, home, or student
type → Mac or PC
operating system (OS) → Mac OS-X Lion, Microsoft Windows, or Linux
screen size → 13,15, or 17 inches
RAM → 2, 4, 6, or 8 GB
hard drive → 250, 320, 512, or 750 GB
processor type: AMD, Celeron, or Intel
processor speed: 1.4, 1.67, or 2.53 GHz
battery: 6 or 12 cell
accessories: carrying case, cleaning kit, privacy screen, external mouse

The Film: *Tagged*

Video Vocabulary

The following words and expressions are used in the video. Study them before watching.

To tag	To put an electronic tag (chip) on someone in order to watch where they go
Disclaimer	A statement in which somebody says that he or she is not connected with or responsible for something, or that he or she does not have any knowledge of it
Microchip (chip)	A very small piece of a material that is a semiconductor, used to carry a complicated electronic circuit
Implant	Something that is put into a person's body during a medical operation
Consent	Agreement about something
Veterinarian (vet)	A person who has been trained in the science of animal medicine, whose job is to treat animals who are sick or injured
Mammals	Animals that give birth to live babies, not eggs, and feed their young on milk
Syringe	A plastic or glass tube with a long hollow needle that is used for putting drugs, etc. into a person's body or for taking a small amount of blood from a person
Tumour	A mass of cells growing in or on a part of the body where they should not, sometimes causing medical problems such as cancer
Scooter	A light motorcycle, usually with small wheels and a curved metal cover at the front to protect the rider's legs

Trade-off	The act of balancing two things that are opposed to each other
Stigmatized	Being treated in a way that makes you feel that you are very bad or unimportant
Commodity	A product or a raw material that can be bought and sold
Hermit	A person who lives a very simple life alone and does not meet or talk to other people

Warm-Up Questions

1. Do you think technology today has made people's lives less private? How?
2. Would you be willing to give up your privacy for social or financial benefits?

Comprehension

Exercise A

In this documentary, we follow Mark Stepanek as he tries to decide whether or not to get a radio-frequency identification (RFID) chip implanted in his hand.

Watch the film once and provide the following information.

1. Give examples of three things with RFID chips in them.

2. How did the 9/11 events inspire VeriChip founders to use RFID for medical purposes?

3. Name three of the things Mark Stepanek would like to do after he inserts an RFID chip in his hand.

4. How did the RFID chip save the life of New Jersey police officer Sergeant Koretsky?

5. How does RFID help people with dementia?

6. According to the film, how many people have received RFID implants at the Alzheimer's community care facility in Florida?

7. According to Kevin Haggerty, the University of Alberta professor, which will be the first three groups of people forced to have tracking microchips or similar tracking devices?

8. Give examples of three other technologies that exist today and can potentially be used to track people.

9. Which of the following is not mentioned in the film as a source of concern or a negative aspect of RFID implants?
   a) possibility of cancer
   b) religious reasons
   c) mind control
   d) tracking and control by marketing companies
   e) tracking and control by governments

10. Which of the following is not mentioned in the film as a benefit of RFID implants?
    a) exchanging information quickly with other people with RFID implants
    b) accessing a person's medical records
    c) finding lost pets
    d) tracking small children or people with memory problems
    e) not carrying lots of keys in your pockets

Exercise B

Now watch the film again and circle *T* if the statement is true or *F* if it is false. Also correct the false statements.

1. The three tags that Mark shows at the beginning of the film are medical RFID chips. T F

2. Dr. Kent Ackerman, the veterinarian, thinks putting implants in people is very different from putting them in pets. T F

3. Peter de Jager believes that there is nothing good or bad about RFID technology. It's what we do with it that matters. T F

4. Amal Graafstra believes that using RFID in humans is not wrong as long as there is consent. T F

5. Scott Silverman, the CEO of VeriChip, believes that chip implants may cause tumours in humans. T F

6. Bob Schiffer, the elderly man with dementia, went to the emergency room after he received his RFID implant. T F

7. Katherine Albrecht believes that the RFID implants could be the evil mark of the beast that was mentioned in the Bible. T F

8. Two doctors and a tattoo artist refused to put the chip in Mark before another piercing artist accepted to do it at Mark's home. T F

9. According to Professor Haggerty, privacy is like a commodity that we give away piece by piece in exchange for benefits. T F

10. Professor Haggerty believes that another reason people might give up their privacy is peer pressure. If everybody else has chips, you feel left out and are forced to get one. T F

Discussion

In teams of two or three, discuss the following question. Take notes based on your discussions as you will be using your notes for the writing exercise that follows.

After having watched the film, do you think having an RFID implant is good or bad overall? Why?

Writing

Would you ever accept to receive an RFID implant? Why? Discuss your reasons for or against an RFID implant in two or three paragraphs.

Reading

Vocabulary

Read the bolded words in context and guess what each one means. You may also refer to the reading passage for more usage examples. The first one has been done as an example.

1. The charitable organization was created with the mandate to protect young children from polio.

   Mandate means *an official instruction given to an organization to do something*.

2. He is in love with hockey. He is a real hockey enthusiast.

   Enthusiast means _____.

3. Be careful when you make major purchases such as a house or a new car.

   Purchase means _____.

4. He read a guidebook on how to conduct business in South Korea and Japan.

   To conduct means _____.

5. iPhone integrates easily with iMac.

   To integrate means _____.

6. I couldn't go to Ottawa to take a tour of the National Gallery, so I took the <u>virtual</u> tour on their website. It's better than nothing.

   Virtual means _____.

7. Bill Gates's career spans four decades.

   To span means _____.

8. When I buy a computer, I value its ease of use and convenience more than its beauty.

   Convenience means _____.

9. When Twitter was first created, nobody thought people would embrace the idea so quickly and widely.

   Embrace means _____.

10. International observers were called in to oversee the elections in Sudan.

    Oversee means _____.

11. He has obeyed all company rules during his long career, but nobody ever seems to notice or appreciate this full compliance.

    Compliance means _____.

12. Facebook was forced to disclose the online identity of a user who posted negative comments about the teenager on her wall.

    To disclose means _____.

13. The government introduced new legislation to protect children online.

    Legislation means _____.

14. My grandfather was a major stakeholder in that company. He owned 30 percent of the company.

    Stakeholder means _____.

15. I'm not a reactive person. I don't wait for bad things to happen and then think of a solution. I plan solutions **proactively**.

    Proactively means _____.

16. The RCMP officers were involved in a **transborder** chase. They followed the criminals inside American borders.

    Transborder means _____.

Warm-Up Questions

1. Have you ever read the terms of use and privacy policies of websites before entering your personal information?
2. Who do you go to if you have a complaint about your privacy rights in Canada?

Louise and David's World

Louise is a 21-year-old college student who likes to meet people and try new things. She is active on-line, using the web for everything from buying clothing and concert tickets to keeping in touch with friends by posting updates and photos to her Facebook page. Now in her final year of college, Louise is starting to look for a job. She is putting herself through school by making jewellery and selling it online. She also collects specialty comic books and belongs to an international network of comic-book **enthusiasts**. Louise has a younger brother, David, who is nine years old. David loves online games and signs up for them on his own, but uses his sister's credit card for any **purchases**.

Now and then, Louise wonders what these online companies do with the information she gives them. She has heard some people talk about "privacy online," but she isn't sure what that means. One time, she noticed a link to a privacy policy on a website. She clicked on it, tried to read it, but became bored with it. It seemed like a bunch of legal talk. She gave up and continued with her activities.

Louise and David are typical Canadians. They are among the millions who connect to the Internet every day to shop, talk to others, play games, or, like Louise, **conduct** business. They see the advantages of life online, and as younger Canadians, Louise and David have **integrated** the **virtual** world into their real-world experiences. They do not remember a time of paper files, typewriters, fold-up maps, or lining up to buy movie tickets. They live an on-demand life, with instant access to all sorts of information—what their friends are up to, where they can find the best deals, and whom their favourite rock star is dating. They run their social lives online; they upload their photographs, videos, and opinions; and they feel part of a community that **spans** the globe. If they are old enough, they pay bills, apply for credit, or run businesses. Music, videos, films, books, clothes, newspapers, and games are a click away. And access to much of this is free, at least in the monetary sense.

Canadians of all ages see the value that technology brings to their lives—**convenience**, connection, creativity—and are **embracing** it. That does not mean, though, that Canadians like Louise never consider what goes on in the background of their web activities. Where does the information go? Who looks at it? Louise seeks answers, but finds information hard to find or confusing and more complex than she thought. Perhaps Louise senses that she is missing the bigger picture. But where can she go to find the "big picture"? The technology is so easy to use, she thinks, so why is it so hard to understand how her personal information fits in?

Fortunately for Louise, there are laws in Canada about how her information is treated, and there is an office that helps **oversee compliance** with those rules. The **mandate** of the Office of the Privacy Commissioner of Canada (OPC) is to oversee compliance with the Privacy Act, which applies to the personal information handling practices of federal government departments and agencies, and the Personal Information Protection and Electronic Documents Act (PIPEDA), Canada's private sector privacy law. PIPEDA applies to organizations that collect, use, and disclose personal information in the course of a commercial activity (unless substantially similar provincial legislation is in place). PIPEDA also covers the personal information of customers and employees of federal works, undertakings, and businesses. Generally speaking, PIPEDA would apply to the personal-information handling practices of private sector organizations engaged in online tracking, profiling and targeting, and cloud computing.

The mission of the OPC is to protect and promote the privacy rights of individuals. To that end, the Office seeks opportunities to promote public awareness and education of privacy rights and obligations through engagement with federal institutions and bodies, the private sector, a wide range of other interested stakeholders, and the public at large. If Louise wanted to, she could visit our website, call us with her questions, or file a complaint if she was concerned about something one of the companies she dealt with was doing. Among its many functions, the OPC investigates complaints; responds to inquiries from individuals, parliamentarians, and organizations seeking information and guidance; proactively engages with stakeholders; provides public education materials and guidance documents; monitors trends; and works with privacy stakeholders from other jurisdictions in Canada and internationally to address global privacy issues that result from ever-increasing transborder data flows.

Comprehension

1. What is the main purpose of this passage?

2. Name four things that Louise does online.

3. What does David usually do online?

4. Why didn't Louise finish reading the privacy terms of the website she was using?

5. Why does this passage tell the story of Louise and David?

6. According to this passage, do Canadians like Louise care where their information goes? How do you know?

7. What is the mandate of the Office of the Privacy Commissioner of Canada (OPC)?

8. What is the difference between the Privacy Act and PIPEDA?

9. Name some of the things that the OPC does for public and private organizations, the federal government, parliamentarians, and the public.

Listening

Vocabulary

The following words and expressions are used in the audio. Study them before listening.

Transparent	Allowing you to see the truth easily
Profiling	The act of collecting useful information about somebody or something so that you can give a description of them or it
Cloud computing	A way of using computers in which data and software are stored mainly on a central computer, to which users have access over the internet
Opt in (to something)	To choose to be part of a system or an agreement
Opt out (of something)	To choose not to take part in something
Backlash	A strong negative reaction by a large number of people; for example, to something that has recently changed in society
Legislate	To create a new law and have it officially accepted
Regulate	To control something by means of rules
Commercial	Connected with the buying and selling of goods and services
Entity	Something that exists separately from other things and has its own identity

Warm-Up Questions

1. Do you think privacy is dead?
2. What kind of people do you think will become happy if privacy is dead?

Post-privacy

Many of us are becoming more comfortable living publicly online, and Christian Heller is an extreme example. For the past year, Christian has been living completely transparently, posting everything about his life on a public wiki. He calls it "post-privacy." Living in such a transparent way brings up all kinds of interesting questions about privacy so Spark called up Canada's privacy commissioner, Jennifer Stoddart who recently released a report on online tracking and targeting.

Exercise A

Listen to the audio clip once and circle *T* if the statement is true or *F* if it is false. Also correct the false statements.

1. Canada's privacy commissioner believes that privacy is dead.   T   F

2. According to Jennifer Stoddart, Canada's privacy commissioner, there is almost nothing that online marketers cannot track.   T   F

3. The commissioner says that most online tracking originates from Europe.   T   F

4. The commissioner believes that online tracking is a danger to our freedom.   T   F

5. The commissioner hopes that the industry will come up with effective self-monitoring codes of practice for its collection of personal information.   T   F

6. The commissioner believes that personal information should only be collected with consent.   T   F

7. The commissioner believes that our present privacy laws are strong enough to protect us.   T   F

8. The commissioner believes that nations do not need to give stronger powers to privacy commissioners.   T   F

9. The commissioner believes that there is not enough investment in online security measures to protect personal information.   T   F

10. The commissioner is trying to make the government approve more serious punishments for companies that mishandle personal information.   T   F

Exercise B

Listen to the clip again and answer the following questions.

1. What kind of people say privacy is dead?

2. Why do they say that privacy is dead?

3. The privacy commissioner's office recently published a report. What was the report about?

4. What are some of the things advertisers and marketers can track online? (Name at least three.)

5. Why is there more online tracking in the United States than in Canada?

6. What will the Canadian information button (the little *i*) do for Canadians?

7. What are some of the new laws Stoddart has asked Parliament to consider passing? (Name at least two.)

8. Who are the two people whom she has consulted about the adequacy of the privacy commissioner's powers?

Idiomatic and Fixed Expressions

The expressions and idioms below are related to caution. Guess each idiom's meaning. Then, check your dictionary to see if you guessed right and write the correct definition in the space provided.

Expression	Meaning
To think twice	
To watch your step	
To play safe	
To look before you leap	
To err on the side of caution	
To cover your tracks	
To tread carefully	
To mind what you are doing	
To keep your back covered	
Once bitten, twice shy	

Speaking

Give Safety Tips and Advice

Work in teams of two. Take turns. Use the idioms on page 191 to give safety tips and advice for each of the following situations. The first one has been done for you as an example.

How to make safe transactions on eBay
How to protect your computer from hackers
How to protect the data on your cellphone
How to protect yourself from identity theft
How to protect your house against burglars
How to protect your car from thieves

Example:

Student A: How can I make safe transactions on eBay?

Student B: Always **think twice** before you send any money. If you are not sure about the seller's reputation, it is always better to **err on the side of caution**. It is also good to **keep your back covered** by paying through PayPal. PayPal insures all transactions and pays back your money if the item is not received or if it is damaged.

Canadian Outlook

Canadians Online

About 70 percent of Canadians are online and according to several studies they spend more time online than users in any other country. Canadian web users are very similar to users in the rest of the world. The most popular sites in Canada are major international ones such as Google and Facebook.

Here are the top ten websites visited by Canadians:

1. Google
2. Facebook
3. YouTube
4. Yahoo!
5. Windows Live

6. Wikipedia
7. Blogger
8. Twitter
9. MSN
10. Kijiji

Discuss why you think Internet use is so high in Canada compared to the rest of the world.

Based on what you learned in this chapter and your personal experience, how much do you think Canadians care about their privacy and safety online?

Writing

Giving Tips to Solve a Problem

Imagine you are a security expert on identity theft. A reporter asked you to provide her readers with specific tips on how to protect the following personal information. Complete the table below by providing two or three solutions or tips for each situation. Then develop each problem and solution into a paragraph. The first one has been done for you as an example.

Things to Protect	How
a) Social insurance number (SIN)	1. Give out your SIN only if legally required. 2. Never carry your SIN card with you. 3. Shred all paper records containing your SIN.
b) Banking and credit information	
c) Personal identity numbers (PIN)	
d) Address and date of birth	

Example:

> Your social insurance number is confidential. You are required to give it to your employer, to your financial institution and accountant for tax purposes, and to the government of Canada to receive services. Do not provide your SIN to people such as your landlord or other businesses and people who are not entitled to it. It is also a good idea to memorize your SIN instead of carrying the card around. Make sure you destroy all documents containing your SIN before putting them in the garbage.

Appendix

Canadian Outlook (p. 114)

Rank	People	Places	Events	Accomplishments	Symbols
1	Pierre Elliott Trudeau	Niagara Falls	Canada Day	Canadarm	Maple leaf
2	Wayne Gretzky	Rocky Mountains	Confederation	Peacekeeping forces	Hockey
3	Terry Fox	Parliament Hill	World Wars	Universal health care	Canadian flag
4	Celine Dion	Ottawa	Calgary Stampede	Discovery of insulin	Beaver
5	Sir John A. Macdonald	CN Tower	Battle of Vimy Ridge	Invention of the telephone	RCMP

Canadian Outlook (p. 133)

Canadian Charter of Rights and Freedoms

Fundamental freedoms	Everyone has the following fundamental freedoms: (a) freedom of conscience and religion; (b) freedom of thought, belief, opinion and expression, including freedom of the press and other media of communication; (c) freedom of peaceful assembly; and (d) freedom of association.
Democratic rights	• Every citizen of Canada has the right to vote in an election of members of the House of Commons or of a legislative assembly and to be qualified for membership therein. • No House of Commons and no legislative assembly shall continue for longer than five years from the date fixed for the return of the writs of a general election of its members. In time of real or apprehended war, invasion or insurrection, a House of Commons may be continued by Parliament and a legislative assembly may be continued by the legislature beyond five years if such continuation is not opposed by the votes of more than one-third of the members of the House of Commons or the legislative assembly, as the case may be. • There shall be a sitting of Parliament and of each legislature at least once every twelve months.
Mobility rights	Every citizen of Canada has the right to enter, remain in and leave Canada. Every citizen of Canada and every person who has the status of a permanent resident of Canada has the right (a) to move to and take up residence in any province; and (b) to pursue the gaining of a livelihood in any province. These rights are subject to (a) any laws or practices of general application in force in a province other than those that discriminate among persons primarily on the basis of province of present or previous residence; and (b) any laws providing for reasonable residency requirements as a qualification for the receipt of publicly provided social services.

Legal rights	• Everyone has the right to life, liberty and security of the person and the right not to be deprived thereof except in accordance with the principles of fundamental justice.
	
	• Everyone has the right to be secure against unreasonable search or seizure.
	
	• Everyone has the right not to be arbitrarily detained or imprisoned.
	
	• Everyone has the right on arrest or detention
	  (a) to be informed promptly of the reasons therefor;
	  (b) to retain and instruct counsel without delay and to be informed of that right; and
	  (c) to have the validity of the detention determined by way of habeas corpus and to be released if the detention is not lawful.
	
	• Any person charged with an offence has the right
	  (a) to be informed without unreasonable delay of the specific offence;
	  (b) to be tried within a reasonable time;
	  (c) not to be compelled to be a witness in proceedings against that person in respect of the offence;
	  (d) to be presumed innocent until proven guilty according to law in a fair and public hearing by an independent and impartial tribunal;
	  (e) not to be denied reasonable bail without just cause;
	  (f) except in the case of an offence under military law tried before a military tribunal, to the benefit of trial by jury where the maximum punishment for the offence is imprisonment for five years or a more severe punishment;
	  (g) not to be found guilty on account of any act or omission unless, at the time of the act or omission, it constituted an offence under Canadian or international law or was criminal according to the general principles of law recognized by the community of nations;
	  (h) if finally acquitted of the offence, not to be tried for it again and, if finally found guilty and punished for the offence, not to be tried or punished for it again; and
	  (i) if found guilty of the offence and if the punishment for the offence has been varied between the time of commission and the time of sentencing, to the benefit of the lesser punishment.
	
	• Everyone has the right not to be subjected to any cruel and unusual treatment or punishment.
	
	• A witness who testifies in any proceedings has the right not to have any incriminating evidence so given used to incriminate that witness in any other proceedings, except in a prosecution for perjury or for the giving of contradictory evidence.
	
	• A party or witness in any proceedings who does not understand or speak the language in which the proceedings are conducted or who is deaf has the right to the assistance of an interpreter.

Equality rights	Every individual is equal before and under the law and has the right to the equal protection and equal benefit of the law without discrimination and, in particular, without discrimination based on race, national or ethnic origin, colour, religion, sex, age or mental or physical disability. This does not preclude any law, program or activity that has as its object the amelioration of conditions of disadvantaged individuals or groups including those that are disadvantaged because of race, national or ethnic origin, colour, religion, sex, age or mental or physical disability.
Language rights*	• English and French are the official languages of Canada and have equality of status and equal rights and privileges as to their use in all institutions of the Parliament and government of Canada. English and French are the official languages of New Brunswick and have equality of status and equal rights and privileges as to their use in all institutions of the legislature and government of New Brunswick. Nothing in this Charter limits the authority of Parliament or a legislature to advance the equality of status or use of English and French. • The English linguistic community and the French linguistic community in New Brunswick have equality of status and equal rights and privileges, including the right to distinct educational institutions and such distinct cultural institutions as are necessary for the preservation and promotion of those communities. The role of the legislature and government of New Brunswick to preserve and promote the status, rights and privileges referred to above is affirmed. • Everyone has the right to use English or French in any debates and other proceedings of Parliament. • The statutes, records and journals of Parliament shall be printed and published in English and French and both language versions are equally authoritative. • Either English or French may be used by any person in, or in any pleading in or process issuing from, any court established by Parliament. • Any member of the public in Canada has the right to communicate with, and to receive available services from, any head or central office of an institution of the Parliament or government of Canada in English or French, and has the same right with respect to any other office of any such institution where (a) there is a significant demand for communications with and services from that office in such language; or (b) due to the nature of the office, it is reasonable that communications with and services from that office be available in both English and French. • Nothing in the above sections abrogates or derogates from any right, privilege or obligation with respect to the English and French languages, or either of them, that exists or is continued by virtue of any other provision of the Constitution of Canada. • Nothing in the above sections abrogates or derogates from any legal or customary right or privilege acquired or enjoyed either before or after the coming into force of this Charter with respect to any language that is not English or French.

*In the Canadian Charter of Rights and Freedoms, the federal language rights described also apply to New Brunswick at the provincial level.

Minority language education rights	• Citizens of Canada
	(a) whose first language learned and still understood is that of the English or French linguistic minority population of the province in which they reside, or
	(b) who have received their primary school instruction in Canada in English or French and reside in a province where the language in which they received that instruction is the language of the English or French linguistic minority population of the province, have the right to have their children receive primary and secondary school instruction in that language in that province.
	Citizens of Canada of whom any child has received or is receiving primary or secondary school instruction in English or French in Canada, have the right to have all their children receive primary and secondary school instruction in the same language.
	The right of citizens of Canada under subsections (1) and (2) to have their children receive primary and secondary school instruction in the language of the English or French linguistic minority population of a province
	(a) applies wherever in the province the number of children of citizens who have such a right is sufficient to warrant the provision to them out of public funds of minority language instruction; and
	(b) includes, where the number of those children so warrants, the right to have them receive that instruction in minority language educational facilities provided out of public funds.

Photo Credits

1 iStockphoto.com/Moodboard_Images

2 (tl-br) *Galileo Demonstrates His Telescope* by H. J. Detouche, Universal History Arc/Maxx Images, iStockphoto.com/skynesher, iStockphoto.com/scotto72, iStockphoto.com/jsmith, iStockphoto.com/vasiliki

3 clipart.com

14 iStockphoto.com/robcocquyt

17 (tl) iStockphoto.com/Krzysztof Walkow, (tr) Mayskyphoto/Shutterstock.com (bl) iStockphoto.com/s5iztok, (bc) iStockphoto.com/drudy1

19 iStockphoto.com/spxChrome

21 clipart.com

22 *Eating Well with Canada's Food Guide*. Health Canada, 2007. Reproduced with the permission of the Minister of Health, 2011

27 clipart.com

30 iStockphoto.com/blackred

39 iStockphoto.com/leonsbox

41 (tl-br) iStockphoto.com/iconogenic, iStockphoto.com/iconogenic, iStockphoto.com/caracterdesign, iStockphoto.com/1001nights

47 Zvonimir Atletic / Shutterstock.com

59 iStockphoto.com/Christopher Futcher

60 iStockphoto.com/Daniel R. Burch

69–70 Film stills taken from *The Necktie*. © 2008 Julie Roy and Michèle Bélanger. All rights reserved.

72 From WHAT COLOR IS YOUR PARACHUTE? By Richard Bolles, copyright © 2009, 2008, 2007, 2006, 2005, 2004, 2003, 2002, 2001, 2000, 1999, 1998, 1997, 1996, 1995, 1994, 1993, 1992, 1991, 1990, 1989, 1988, 1987, 1986, 1985, 1984, 1983, 1982, 1981, 1980, 1979, 1978, 1977, 1976, 1975, 1972, 1970 by Richard Nelson Bolles. Used by permission of Ten Speed Press, and imprint of the Crown Publishing Group, a division of Random House, Inc.

74 iStockphoto.com/Stephan Hoerold

77 iStockphoto.com/Vasiliki Varvaki

86 (t) Simon Fraser/Science Photo Library, © DEMENTIA EDUCATION AND TRAINING PROGRAM

90 (l) iStockphoto.com/DSGpro (r) iStockphoto.com/blackred

97 (tl-br) iStockphoto.com/Bruce Smith, iStockphoto.com/dwowens, iStockphoto.com/Sang Nguyen, iStockphoto.com/Habman_18

108 *Demasduit* by Lady Henrietta Martha Hamilton, 1819, Library and Archives Canada, acc. no. 1977-14-1

109 Image extracted from "A sketch of the River Exploits and the east end of Lieutenants Lake in Newfoundland [cartographic material] " by John Cartwright. Retrieved from Library and Archives Canada, NMC 27

116 iStockphoto.com/Chris Schmidt

124 iStockphoto.com/Mark Stay

126 clipart.com

135 iStockphoto.com/Marina Bartel

141 clipart.com

156 Source: Harrendorf, S., Heiskanen, M., & Malby, S., International Statistics on Crime and Justice, European Institute for Crime Prevention and Control, affiliated with the United Nations, Helsinki 2010. Figure 4, p 13

157 Source: Harrendorf, S., Heiskanen, M., & Malby, S., International Statistics on Crime and Justice, European Institute for Crime Prevention and Control, affiliated with the United Nations, Helsinki 2010. Table 7, p 106

159 X-ray: NASA/CXC/CfA/E. O'Sullivan Optical: Canada-France-Hawaii-Telescope/Coelum

163 From *Asteroids, Meteorites, and Comets* by Linda T. Elkins-Tanton published by Facts On File, Inc., an imprint of Infobase Publishing

176 Courtesy of Amal Graafstra (www.amal.net)

Literary Credits

13 Excerpts p. 31 from STRATEGIES FOR SUCCESS: A PRACTICAL GUIDE TO LEARNING ENGLISH by H. Douglas Brown. Copyright © 2002 by Addison Wesley Longman.

17 Based on information from *Frommer's 500 Adrenaline Adventures* by Friedland, L., Lallanilla, M., Swetzoff, J., & O'Malley, C. (Frommers, 2010)

22–23 *Eating Well with Canada's Food Guide*. Health Canada, 2007. Reproduced with the permission of the Minister of Health, 2011.

34 *Body Image* edited by Heidi Williams, and published by Greenhaven Press, a part of Gale Cengage Learning 2009. pp. 92–94.

38 Source: Statistics Canada's Health in Canada web portal, Check-up on Canada's health, http://www4.statcan.gc.ca/health-sante/index-eng.htm, Aug 31, 2011

51 MaryRM [pseud], comment on "The Colour of Beauty", comment posted 13 May 2010. http://www.nfb.ca/film/colour_of_beauty/ [accessed Aug 16 2011]. AND Olen [pseud], comment on "The Colour of Beauty", comment posted 20 May 2010. http://www.nfb.ca/film/colour_of_beauty/ [accessed Aug 16 2011].

53 Adapted from Wang, Lu-in. *Discrimination by Default: How Racism Becomes Routine*. p. 3 © 2006 by New York University. All Rights Reserved.

56 Projections of the Diversity of the Canadian Population, 2006 to 2031 (91-551-XWE), March 9, 2010. http://www.statcan.gc.ca/daily-quotidien/100309/dq100309a-eng.htm

56–57 Statistics from http://www.statcan.gc.ca/pub/85f0033m/85f0033m2008017-eng.pdf, http://www.statcan.gc.ca/daily-quotidien/100614/dq100614b-eng.htm, and http://www.statcan.gc.ca/daily-quotidien/100309/dq100309a-eng.htm

57–58 *Black Like Me* by John Howard Griffin was originally published in 1961 by Houghton Mifflin.

61 Based on information from http://islandreefjob.com.au/about-the-best-job/, http://www.digitaljournal.com/article/272163, and http://news.bbc.co.uk/2/hi/8035168.stm. All retrieved Sep. 5, 2011

62 Abridged and adapted from "Best job in the world took its toll on tired Briton" by Bonnie Malkin, 2 January 2010. © Telegraph Media Group Limited 2010.

70–71 From WHAT COLOR IS YOUR PARACHUTE? By Richard Bolles, copyright © 2009, 2008, 2007, 2006, 2005, 2004, 2003, 2002, 2001, 2000, 1999, 1998, 1997, 1996, 1995, 1994, 1993, 1992, 1991, 1990, 1989, 1988, 1987, 1986, 1985, 1984, 1983, 1982, 1981, 1980, 1979, 1978, 1977, 1976, 1975, 1972, 1970 by Richard Nelson Bolles. Used by permission of Ten Speed Press, and imprint of the Crown Publishing Group, a division of Random House, Inc.

75 Speaking Exercise A is based on an exercise from *Conversation Gambits: Real English Conversation Practices* by Eric Keller and Sylvia Warner. (England: Language Teaching Publications, 1988. p. 79)

80 Reprinted with permission from *Britannica Student Encyclopedia*, © 2010 by Encyclopaedia Britannica, Inc.

83–84 The text used in Exercise C was adapted and abridged from *Creative Visualization* by Shakti Gawain (Novato CA: New World Library, 1998. pp x–xi)

95 Based on information from http://braincanada.ca/files/case_news_release.pdf and http://www.cmha.ca/data/1/rec_docs/155_mental_illnessENG.pdf. Both accessed June 11, 2011

99–100 © Citizenship and Immigration Canada. Reproduced with the permission of the Minister of Public Works and Government Services Canada (2011). Source: Library and Archives Canada/*A Newcomer's Introduction to Canada, 2003*/AMICUS 32464245/Pages 26 and 27

108–09 "The Story of Demasduit (Mary March)" in *Canada: A People's History Volume One* by Don Gillmor and Pierre Turgeon. Copyright © 2001 by Canadian Broadcasting Corporation. Published by McClelland & Stewart Ltd. Used with permission from the publisher.

117 Sources: Tarantino, B. *Under Arrest: Canadian Laws You Won't Believe* (Toronto: Dundurn Press, 2007), http://hubpages.com/hub/101-Strangest-Laws-From-Around-The-World, and http://www.lufa.ca/news/news_item.asp?NewsID=7235

118 Sources: *Civil Resistance and Power Politics: The Experience of Non-violent Action from Gandhi to the Present* Eds. Adam Roberts & Timothy Garton Ash (New York: Oxford University Press, 2009) and *Path of Resistance: the Practice of Civil Disobedience* by Per Herngren (Philidephia PA: New Society Publishers, 1993)

128–29 From *Small Acts of Resistance: How Courage, Tenacity, and Ingenuity Can Change the World* © 2008 by Steve Crawshaw and John Jackson. Used with permission by Sterling Publishing Co., Inc.

162 Adapted with permission from *Exploring Space: Journey Through the Solar System and Beyond*, © 2008 by Encyclopedia Britannica, Inc.

170–71 Adapted and abridged from The Future of the Universe by Jack Meadows © Springer-Verlag London (pp 81, 85, 86 and 95) with kind permission from Springer Science+Business Media B.V.

172–73 NASA/JPL-Caltech

179 From *Privacy in the Information Age* by Harry Henderson published by Facts On File, Inc., an imprint of Infobase Publishing, pp. 4–5

188 Source: Report on the 2010 Office of the Privacy Commissioner of Canada's Consultations on Online Tracking, Profiling and Targeting, and Cloud Computing, Privacy Commissioner of Canada, 2011

189–90 Intro to Post-privacy adapted and abridged from http://www.cbc.ca/spark/2011/06/spark-152-june-19-22-2011/

194 (top) Information retrieved from "Canadians Choose the People, Places, Events, Accomplishments and Symbols that Define Canada" © Ipsos Reid. http://www.dominion.ca/Canada101.pdf